Act Yourself

THE TRANSFORMATION SERIES
Gay Hendricks, *General Editor*

Books in The Transformation Series
explore the transitions of human life
and the possibilities for happier,
more creative living through the
application of the psychology of adjustment.

Other books in the series:

How to Love Every Minute of Your Life
by Gay Hendricks and Carol Leavenworth

I Know What's Wrong,
But I Don't Know What to Do About It
by Arnold P. Goldstein, Robert P. Sprafkin, and N. Jane Gershaw

The Family Centering Book:
Awareness Activities the Whole Family
Can Do Together
by Gay Hendricks

Talk to Yourself: Using the Power of Self-Talk
by Charles Zastrow

Divorce: How and When to Let Go
by Nancy Adam and John Adam

You're Divorced, But Your Children Aren't
by T. Roger Duncan and Darlene Duncan

JO LOUDIN is a therapist in private practice, and she teaches human relations courses in colleges and for government and private industry. A specialist in communications in human relationships, she has extensive background in Gestalt therapy, drama therapy, psychodrama, and Transactional Analysis.

Act Yourself

stop playing roles and unmask your true feelings

Jo Loudin

A SPECTRUM BOOK

PRENTICE-HALL, INC., *Englewood Cliffs, New Jersey 07632*

Library of Congress Cataloging in Publication Data

LOUDIN, JO.
  Act yourself.

  (The Transformation series) (A Spectrum Book)
  Bibliography: p.
  Includes index.
  1. Success. 2. Interpersonal relations.
3. Expression. 4. Role playing. I. Title.
BF637.S8L598   158   79-4245
ISBN 0-13-003715-X
ISBN 0-13-003707-9 pbk.

Editorial/production supervision and
  interior design by Carol Smith
Cover design by Graphikann
Manufacturing buyer: Cathie Lenard

© 1979 by Prentice-Hall, Inc. *Englewood Cliffs, New Jersey 07632*

A SPECTRUM BOOK

10 9 8 7 6 5 4 3 2 1

Printed in the United States of America

PRENTICE-HALL INTERNATIONAL, INC., *London*
PRENTICE-HALL OF AUSTRALIA PTY. LIMITED, *Sydney*
PRENTICE-HALL OF CANADA, LTD., *Toronto*
PRENTICE-HALL OF INDIA PRIVATE LIMITED, *New Delhi*
PRENTICE-HALL OF JAPAN, INC., *Tokyo*
PRENTICE-HALL OF SOUTHEAST ASIA PTE. LTD., *Singapore*
WHITEHALL BOOKS LIMITED, *Wellington, New Zealand*

To Sunny,
through whose eyes
I learned to see.

Contents

Acknowledgments

I am very grateful to all the people who have given me encouragement during the writing of this book. I thank my husband, Ralph, for the support he has given me, the housework and babysitting he has shared so that I could work. I thank Sharon Roberts for her constructive criticism. Marilyn Neal deserves special thanks for her judicious comments about the manuscript and her careful typing of it. I am grateful to Mark Harris, master of the English language, for his meticulous editing of my otherwise sprawling book.

Acknowledgment is made to the International Transactional Analysis Association and Stephen Karpman for permission to reprint the drawing of the Drama Triangle by Stephen Karpman, M.D., from his article entitled "Fairytales and Script Drama Analysis" from *Vol. 7, No. 26*, April 1968; and to Prentice-Hall, Inc. for permission to adapt material from *A New Guide to Rational Living* by Albert Ellis, Ph.D. and Robert A. Harper, Ph.D.

Above all, I am deeply appreciative of the hundreds of people I have worked with over the past ten years in classes and therapy sessions, some of whom have created the content of the book. These people came to me to better understand themselves, yet I feel that I got more than I gave, for I have gained much self-understanding from them. In this book, which wrote itself as much as it was written, I wish to pass on to you, the reader, the understanding that I gained from these people.

Introduction

This book is about roles and why people play them. It is also about how to stop playing them and start being yourself—not the self you have been taught to act, nor the self you think you should act, but the real You that is contained in the center of your being, the You that is okay, perfect, and complete within yourself. If you can accept yourself as inherently perfect, you can stop struggling to become the impossible fantasy of yourself you have been trying so hard to achieve. You can stop living up to others' expectations of what you should be and start living your life as *You* want.

You do not *have* to act any particular role or roles; you *choose* to do so. The reasons for your choosing to act these roles are involved with your basic needs for survival as a person. If you can understand the reasons behind your choice of roles and make new decisions concerning your real survival needs, you can start to live a different kind of life. If you can start to believe at an emotional level that you will survive as You even if you stop acting your old role, then you can drop the old familiar but destructive ways of thinking, feeling, and behaving. You can decide to risk being yourself and live the happy, healthy, and fulfilled life you have always wanted.

Early in life each person is given a role to act out. Each role has rules behind it to specify how it should be played. Even in the cradle infants learn rules from their parents, and they make certain decisions concerning how they will play the role. Their decisions, though unspoken and at a subconscious level, may affect them for the rest of their lives. Let's say, for example, that a baby boy gets no response when he cries from hunger but is kept on a strict feeding schedule. He may decide it does no good to communicate his needs to others. If he is raised rigidly in other ways, he may follow up this early decision by choosing to close himself off from others. As he grows older he continues to make decisions which affect his attitudes and behavior. He learns that he should be brave and strong, a "tough guy" on whom women can lean. He gets attention, bad or good, for his rebelliousness and a certain acceptance of his rowdiness: "Boys will be boys."

The little girl whose mother responds to smiles and coos but will not permit rebelliousness may smile her way through life as a "nice" girl, letting others walk all over her. She learns, on the other hand, that she should be nice, act like a "lady," not be too smart, and do for others. She is not encouraged to be aggressive, told instead when she feels angry, "Ladies don't get mad."

These boys and girls do not have to accept these roles. They may decide to rebel. In that case societal inhibitors will pressure them to conform. The boy who decides to become a ballet dancer or the girl who wants to be a fire fighter may be ridiculed by disapproving classmates and relatives. So most young people decide to accept their roles rather than fight. Certainly it is easier today than it was even ten years ago to do your own thing, but societal pressure still exists in subtle forms and usually only the nonconformist manages to evade the given roles.

Those who conform to their roles in life may find themselves as grownups feeling frustrated, bored, unfulfilled, and sometimes terribly depressed without knowing why. They have played by the rules and are living the roles. Why then are they not content? Women are starting to verbalize their sense of discontent lately because of the emphasis on liberation. Frustration drives many women into a search for identity. "I don't know who I am anymore," one woman told me recently. "I've been a wife, mother, housekeeper, chauffeur, cook, and cleaning lady for everybody else for so long, there's no *me* left." Many men are also becoming aware of their discontent, whether or not they verbalize it. Many would secretly like to get off the treadmill, stop working, and get some fun out of life. Is it any wonder that many husbands—and wives—one day simply disappear?

There are, of course, fortunate boys and girls. These children have been raised by parents who view them as people with feelings and opinions of their own. These boys and girls are permitted to be themselves. They are encouraged to feel what they feel and to ask for what they want. They also grow up and find themselves expected to fit into cultural roles. Societal messages remind them of these roles. I heard one such message a few months ago. My daughter had given a toy to a three-year-old girl. When the child did not say "Thank you," her aunt said, at least five times, "Kathy, nice girls say 'Thank you.' Be a nice girl now and say 'Thank you' for the gift." That message, given often enough over the years, could program the child into compliance with the "nice girl" role. Or, she might decide that she was not a "nice girl." Therefore she might decide to be bad and play out a "bad girl" role for the rest of her life.

Unlike this little girl, fortunate children are taught that it is okay to be themselves and ignore society's messages. They still encounter problems; they still get angry and hurt, and they feel bad occasionally. But these children, unlike the others, do not become as incapacitated by life's problems. They know the joy and fulfillment that the others miss. They dare to risk knowing their own potential. And in their brief sojourn on this earth they experience their own and others' humanness to the full.

I am not speaking of a lot of unknown "theys." I am speaking about myself and about many others—men and women—whom I have known through teaching and working as a group and individual therapist. I know from my own experience and theirs that even if a person spends most of his or her life being a loser, that person can change the attitudes of a lifetime, change his or her behavior accordingly, and enjoy a life of self-fulfillment.

I believe that both men and women can live fuller lives if they free themselves from restrictive roles and express their feelings. Men are generally expected to be strong and silent; they need permission to openly communicate their feelings of pain, tenderness, fear, and loneliness. Women generally need permission to express anger directly and verbally. I also believe that women have farther to go in becoming themselves than men, who have been given more freedom culturally to do things and be somebody and move about in the world.

I first became aware of the limitations of American roles in the fifties when I worked with the YWCA. I repeatedly heard young women complaining about being "housewives," but at that time I had no concept of their problems. It was not until years later when I experienced marriage, motherhood, and the isolation of being a housewife in suburbia that I understood. Then I found myself yearning for some sense of identity apart from my home—some sense of being "me" apart from "wife and mother." Being "just a housewife" was totally dissatisfying to me.

Of course, that is not to put down being a housewife. Today, may women feel pressured to get a job even though they would rather be homemakers. If they truly find fulfillment in their homemaking, I say "Fine!" I dislike pressure to conform to any arbitrary role. As a "people's libber," I am committed to freedom of choice, provided it is not harmful to others. I believe that both women and men should be allowed to do what they want to do. Let each be housewife or househusband, jobholder or flower child without being rebuked for that choice.

Recently certain writers have tried to reinforce traditional wifely roles by preaching increased subservience to men. These books primarily teach women how to expertly manipulate their mates. Now, I have nothing against manipulation. With awareness of what you are doing, it simply becomes one more tool to use in relating to people. *Without* awareness you may become stuck in your manipulation, unable to be intimate at all. Manipulation, therefore, should be recognized as a secondary approach within a relationship. If you cannot get what you want by being open and intimate, you may have no other choice. But if you use manipulation as a primary mode of behavior, you will find intimacy impossible to achieve.

What is intimacy? When I use the term, I do not mean sexuality, although that may be a part of it. I mean being open, taking the risk of being hurt by communicating openly and truthfully with another. I mean bringing innermost feelings to light—expressing thoughts and feelings without hedging, without editing, and as directly as language permits. And I mean expressing oneself not only to family members but to strangers, or perhaps the other way around, because it is often easier to express feelings to someone you will never meet again.

I remember a workshop leader saying once, "You cannot *not* communicate." Others become aware of the messages you are sending out no matter how hard you try to conceal your real feelings. You communicate your sense of isolation just as you communicate your willingness to be close. Intimacy is closeness. Intimacy is the willingness to reach out and touch another person either physically or verbally in the here and now. When you are intimate you accept another as he or she *is* and not as some fantasized ideal." You see and appreciate another as a unique human being without trying to change that person to fit your mold. You hear the words that person speaks and you feel the impact of his or her words upon you. You feel that the other person hears *you*.

When you are intimate you communicate to another what you are feeling within your body. If you are not in touch with your feelings—if you are not self-intimate first—you will find it difficult to be intimate with others. You will also find it difficult to be in touch with your own sexuality, for after all, sexual feelings are feelings too. That is, you may have sex continually to release bodily tension and still miss deep sexual fulfillment.

I have heard a familiar complaint from many women over the years: "My husband wants sex all the time but he won't ever tell me what he feels." Equally familiar to me is the complaint from men: "My wife wants me to hold her and talk to her before she'll have sex with me. When I don't say the right words she gets mad and there's no sex. I don't know what she wants to hear." What does the woman want to hear? What are the "right words"? I have no pat answer for what a man should say to a woman. I do know that she does not want to hear a discourse on what she should or shouldn't feel, or the latest business deal, or his opinions on the state of the world. She does want to hear him speak of what he feels; she wants to respond with her real feelings.

The problem men have in conveying their feelings is that they have been role-trained not to feel. They have been told from infancy on, "Boys don't cry," "Don't be a sissy," "Don't be scared," "Be a tough little man," and thousands of similar messages so often that they literally have lost touch with their feelings. I remember once asking a client of mine, "What are you feeling?" He said, "You know, I've got this lump down here in my stomach, a whole mess of feelings, but damned if I know what they are." In order to discover what they are, this man would have to let go of the messages in his head about not feeling and get in touch with his own feelings, his own pain. Let's face it, feelings are not always joyous. They can hurt. How many men and women are willing to put aside their defenses, built up over a lifetime, and get in touch with their pain?

On rereading this last paragraph I see the word "feeling" appear over and over again. It sounds as though I am talking to a client. When I am working in a therapy session, I hear myself repeatedly asking "What are you feeling?" A few nights ago in group therapy, I struggled with my fatigue none too successfully. When I fell asleep a group member yelled, "Wake up, Jo, I want you to hear this." As I jerked awake I had a fantasy that I had fallen asleep and the entire group tip-toed silently out of the room. In my fantasy I awoke and said to the empty room, "What are you feeling?"

It's my one-liner. If I did not have it I would be tongue-tied. Some have accused me of having a limited vocabulary, and I admit that I do. Oh, I change it once in a while to "What are you experiencing?" or "What's happening with you?" But my meaning is essentially the same: "What's going on in your body?" and "Where in your body are you experiencing pain?"

Intimacy also means being able to take as well as to give. Women in particular have been trained to give to others regardless of their own desires. When they think about buying something or taking time for themselves, they have a vague sense of guilt. They should, they believe, think of others first. So they strain to give to their families and friends, and the more they give, the more they resent giving. These women need to ask for what they themselves want, even though they may at first encounter their own guilt. They need to take the risk of being refused when they ask. They also need to risk revealing *all* of their feelings openly; even though women have generally been given permission to feel more than men, they have been role-trained to repress some of their feelings. They have been taught that if they express anger they will hurt someone ("Ladies don't get mad."). So they hold their anger inside. They have been taught that they should not refuse anyone, so they continue to say "yes" to others sweetly—and resentfully.

Men, for their part, have been role-trained to protect women. They have been taught that they should repress their pain, their fear, and their sense of inadequacy in order to appear strong and resourceful. They have learned to hide their "weaknesses" in order that women might feel secure. And they have been taught to believe that they should not express their resentments or they will hurt the feelings of their women. Men do have more permission to be aggressive, but many of them have been taught to initially repress their feelings, hurting inside, resenting in silence, letting their anger build up until they explode outwardly or push their emotions down and into long-lasting pain.

If men and women continue to hold in their anger, give to others with resentment, and protect others out of their own pain, how can they become more intimate? If intimacy means openness, resentment means the opposite—erecting barriers and withholding confidences. I know that if I resent someone I do not want to expose my innermost self to that person. I close myself off from that person. And if I am not asking for what I want out of life, my resentment may be entirely of my own making. How much better to feel that I deserve life; I have a right to ask for what I want from life and get it. Then I can be in touch with my own power. I know I can be who I am and survive. I can risk revealing myself to another person in intimacy. I also know that I do not have to be "nice" and hide my real feelings from another, that I can express anger or fear or hurt without feeling responsible for another's feelings. Nor do I have to accept guilt if that person tries to "make me feel" guilty for my openness. And he or she can express feelings as openly with me without my reacting defensively.

In a relationship in which the male is dominant and the female submissive, resentments can build up at the price of intimacy. Certainly a man may like being adulated by a subservient wife for a while, but that position can become uncomfortable. As master of the household he will feel important for a time, while she will feel protected. Sooner or later, however, he will make decisions that she does not like. Instead of taking responsibility for her own decisions, she will blame him and will resent complying with his "wrong" decisions. He, in turn, will resent her lack of faith. If their mutual resentment is not expressed, the relationship may become destructive for both partners. One person may submit to total domination by the other, or, as so many couples do today, they may stop trying and get a divorce.

Until they come to some decision, they will live together resentfully. She may begin to feel trapped in her protected cage and lose respect for her "master." Her anger will sneak out in subtle ways. She might burn his toast or lose interest in cleaning the house or, more commonly, turn off sexually. How can two people make love if they are angry at each other? They cannot. So the anger will stay hidden except for those occasions when the partners make covert jabs at each other—perhaps expressing this anger only when other people are around, or ridiculing each other sarcastically and, upon confrontation whipping the anger back under wraps with "What's the matter, can't you take a joke?"

If the resentments remain hidden and unexpressed, even more resentments are generated. A woman in one of my groups, aware of her manipulations, said to me, "No matter how badly I treat my husband, he will take it. Even if he gets fed up and threatens to leave I can twist him around my little finger by shedding a few tears. I can't respect a man who lets me treat him like that!" I have heard other women express their contempt for the "little boys" they married, complaining bitterly that there are no "real men" left in the world. They would not want to admit, however, that they are as much the cause of their sterile relationships as are their men.

The man may feel trapped in another way. He may try very hard to be strong and make the right decisions. If he allows himself to express fear or to fail, both he and his wife may think he is "weak." So he may push himself into an early heart attack or tension headaches or ulcers, taking his feelings out on his own body. Or he may keep his anger hidden except for occasional explosions when he gets drunk, beats his wife or his kids, smashes up his car, or kills somebody. Other men do none of these things; but quietly, and without any seeming anger, they leave their jobs, their homes, their marriages. Suddenly they are gone with no explanation or understanding for those left behind. They may marry again, probably women much like their former wives, and encounter problems similar to those they experienced in their first marriages. If they do not learn to relate openly with their new mates they will still be closed off, unable to communicate or touch or truly love.

I am not surprised that crime and violence are on the rise in America. Traditional roles have lost their power to hold emotions in check. Underemployment, early retirement, and increased leisure are giving us more opportunity to focus attention on our poverty-stricken relationships. Because of the mounting frustrations, anxiety, and alienation of our highly mobile society, men and women are groping for new roles to fill their needs. We cannot rely on our old roles any longer. We need to reexamine those roles carefully to test their validity in today's society. If the roles we have been trained to act out no longer apply, let's discard them. We need to allow ourselves to express our innermost feelings openly and freely. If we must have roles at all, let them be roles that permit us to be who we are and express what we feel, to enable us to reach out with trust and love—with intimacy.

Communicating openly with another person is risky when we know that we might be misinterpreted, put down, or even worse, ignored. Attempting *anything* is risky, knowing that we might fail. Unfortunately, the way we learn as human beings is by making mistakes, evaluating our errors, and trying again. If we are afraid to take risks we may never do anything. We may end up in the one totally safe place—the grave—without ever having known the satisfaction of accomplishment, shared with anyone intimately, or felt the joy of just being alive. So come along with me. Take the risk of learning how to change your role. Decide to risk becoming You.

I am taking a risk in writing this book. If I worried too much about the opinions of other people I would never write anything. I admit that at times I have thought, "Who am I to write a book when so many others know so much more than I?" If I listened to that message long enough I would never write one paragraph. I would cop out by thinking that if I wanted to, I could write a book that people would like. But I would not risk actually writing it. So instead of listening to my fantasies, I turn on the "I'm okay" message and keep on writing. If much of what I have to say has been said before in different words, it doesn't matter. My words might be more clearly understood than those of others. If they aren't and some people do not understand me or have differing beliefs, I will not crumble. They have a right to their opinions just as I do. I will not limit what I say because I fear adverse opinion or indifference. You may not like my opinions and you are still okay with me.

I can accept your dislike, even of me, because basically I know that I am okay. Even when I do something dumb or silly or even mean, I believe I am inherently okay. Sometimes when I am feeling very small or scared or hurt, I say this over and over to myself to convince myself that I am okay. I said this to a client recently and she said, "You may believe yourself when you say that, but I can't because I know I'm not."

"Say it again then," I said. "Sometimes you need to say it a dozen times before you start to believe it."

"I still wouldn't be able to believe it," she said.

"Then lie a little," I replied. "You've got to start somewhere! And as long as you're lying, make it a good one. Say—I'm fantastic, I'm terrific, I'm grrrrreat!"

"Well, I can't lie that much," she conceded, "but I will start saying I'm okay. I do have to start somewhere."

It is also okay to take the risk of being intimate without manipulating. This is very easy to say and very hard to do. It is threatening to express gut-level feelings with total openness when you are not sure how the other person will receive them. I have heard this fear expressed over and over by men and women in my classes and groups: "If I tell him (her) how I feel I may hurt his (her) feelings." What I hear them really saying is "If I tell him (her) how I feel he (she) may not like me and *I* might get hurt." That is absolutely right. The other person may not like you and may, moreover, reject you. And you might feel hurt because being rejected is painful. So in order to be open with your feelings you have to decide— and no one else can make this decision for you—that if some do not like you and reject you because of it, you will still survive.

In reality you know that everyone in the whole world will not like you. You also know that you do not like every person in this world. You feel uncomfortable around some people and would rather avoid them if you could. So why keep trying to make these people like you when you cannot honestly make yourself care for them? It is your decision. If you feel that you cannot survive—and this is a survival issue—then go on hiding your true feelings and playing your role, whatever it may be.

If, on the other hand, you believe that you are okay without relying on others to convince you that you are, you also know that you will survive being disliked or rejected. So what is stopping you? Go ahead and express your feelings. If you can tell others all of your feelings openly and without hedging for fear of their rejection, if you can allow others to have and express all of their feelings, then truly you can *be* the Self you want to be and *love* the Self you are.

1

Some personal history

If I can make it,
so can you.

I have not always felt okay. In fact, there have been times in years past when I wondered if I ever would. Everyone else seemed to feel 100 percent okay. Even the books I read were written by okay people who seemed to have had loving parents, stable marriages, and neat friends throughout their exciting, enjoyable, fun-filled lives. If they had not had lives like these, they did not mention the fact. I remember feeling discouraged when I thought about all these okay people writing books on how I could feel better about my not-okay self. I thought, "But they don't know! How could they know? They haven't been there!" Well, believe me, I know because I have been there. And I now suspect that they also know, or they could not write books about how you can feel better about yourself. How would they know about feeling better unless they had felt worse? How could they understand negative feelings in other people unless they had had some of their own?

I cannot be sure about the negative events and feelings in the personal lives of other authors unless they choose to tell me about them, and most do not. I do know about my own. I choose to share my past, my experiences, and my hangups because I am not comfortable on a pedestal. Some people have placed me on that pedestal because they see me only in the authoritative roles of teacher and therapist. They expect me to be all-knowing and perfect, and they express surprise at my fallibility. But being human is being fallible, and I like being a member of the human race. Maintaining distance will not get me into the club of humanity. The badge of membership, unfortunately, is fear, hurt, and pain. If I show my badge to you, you may feel freer to open yourself to me and reveal yours.

I remember one woman who took a class of mine and saw me as more than human. Either I did little sharing in that class, or else she did not hear what I revealed about myself. When she came to my home later to participate in a group she said, "Jo, it's so nice to see you as an ordinary person. Somehow I never thought you'd have a bathroom in your house!"

"How 'bout that," I laughed. "I'm a real human being!" Yet, I knew what she meant. I have felt awed by some authority figures. Somehow they seemed larger than life. Now I know they are really not. They are the same as the rest of us. If they are open about their own suffering they will reveal themselves as bona fide members—as I do.

I wear my membership badge not proudly but openly. I have known depression, anxiety, frustration, insecurity, and a low sense of self-esteem. I have known poverty, divorce, failure. From years of behaving in a self-defeating way, feeling unloved, and putting myself down, I have finally reached a point where I can say at least 90 percent of the time "I like myself because I am me." The other 10 percent of the time I can tolerate myself because I believe it is okay to feel bad. But most of the time I can recognize depression when it starts and stay out of it. By doing what feels right for me I can enjoy my life. Considering where I have been and where I am now, all I can say is if I can make it, so can you.

It's not that my parents meant to raise an unhappy child, it was just that they did not know how to accept my feelings. They had not been taught that feelings were okay. So they gave me messages they had learned from their parents and their parents before them; how could they know any other way? They taught me, verbally and nonverbally, what they themselves had been taught in childhood: "Children should not get mad; children should love and obey their parents." They did not accept my rebellious feelings because they had been taught that anger is wrong. The more they told me to be nice, and to behave, the more sullen and resentful I became.

They did not know how to express their anger to me other than in commands, mostly "Don'ts." So when they were angry with me but did not tell me straight out and in words that I could understand, I thought that I was to blame, that I was wrong, even that I was bad. Nor did I understand their ways of expressing love. When they tried to show their love indirectly by doing things for me or giving me money and gifts, I felt unloved. If they said, "I love you," I did not hear it. Consequently, I was unhappy much of the time.

My parents had other problems. They were young, both barely into their twenties, and had not expected a child so soon. I was born in 1932, during the worst of the Great Depression. My parents have told me that jobs were almost nonexistent then. There were times when they had no money. They blamed each other for much of what was happening to them. They were going through the financial panic that so many other families shared at that time and the future seemed bleak. They also had religious beliefs to fight against. Through their religion, they had been taught that many of their feelings and their thoughts were sinful, as well as their actions. When their relationship became strained, they blamed themselves for their troubles as much as they blamed each other. I even felt that they blamed me. I do not know whether or not they actually blamed me. I do know that I assumed a great deal of guilt, believing that I was the cause of many of their problems.

During this time I felt small and helpless and often lonely. I also felt frightened. These were valid feelings at that time. I was small and helpless. I had little understanding of our circumstances so, not knowing, I felt afraid. When my parents left me alone or with relatives I felt abandoned. Being an only child, I had few friends my own age around. When I got angry at my parents I had no one to whom I could say "They're being mean," and hear a consoling "They sure are!" coming back to me. Instead, I learned to keep my feelings to myself and I was confused about them.

Because their problems seemed insurmountable my parents eventually got divorced. Both later remarried. I felt guilty about the divorce, somehow to blame. I remember once a priest bawled me out for having a different name from that of my mother, and my sense of guilt increased. It was not okay then to be the child of divorced parents. I felt that not only they, but I too, had sinned.

It was not okay to feel, nor was it okay to express my feelings. I was afraid to ever tell Mom I was angry at her because I had been taught that children should love their parents. I rarely got in touch with my anger toward Dad because if I tried to tell him what I was feeling he joked about it. I did not feel okay about asking for what I wanted because I had been told "Your parents know what's best for you." And I heard "Act your age" and "Don't be silly" so much over the years that I began to feel very awkward about playing freely. Later in my life I learned to bury my anger so effectively that I would carry grudges for years. Instead of being open with my feelings I would direct my hidden anger toward myself, while still feeling resentment toward the other person. Not only did I not ask for what I wanted, I rarely had any idea of what I wanted. I remember wondering how other people could form opinions while I seemed to have none. As for being silly—never! I felt clumsy and embarrassed if someone wanted me to play without purpose. More and more I retreated into the safety of grown-up-ness and work—whether it be work as work or work as play. When I was sixteen, my not-okay child really took over. I rebelled against both my parents and their religion. They both became angry at me. At that time I decided (as I had probably done earlier) that I would make it on my own. That decision, valid at the time for my own survival, led to more feelings of loneliness and alienation. I thought I had forever alienated them. Whatever self-confidence I possessed ebbed away. I became then, and for many years to come, an exile in an unknown land—rootless, driven, and alone.

I suddenly felt as if I had no home with either of my parents. I decided to go away to college. Although I had been an honor student in high school I never considered asking for a scholarship. I did not believe I deserved one. So I worked my way through college, fighting my constant companions—depression and fatigue. Of course I graduated; it never occurred to me *not* to. I also never considered what I would do with the degree afterward. I had vacillated between English and sociology, finally getting a B.A. in English. So I jumped around from one job to another. I was a secretary, a dishwasher, bookkeeper, a waitress, and a stewardess. I married not because I wanted to but because I thought my parents would approve—in 1953 it was not okay to live with someone until you got to know each other. Marriage came first, and if that did not work there was always the escape of divorce. My first marriage lasted ten months. I find it hard to remember much about it other than the fact that we were both unhappy most of the time. In fact, most of what I remember about my past is unhappiness: fear, anxiety, depression, worry—a great black cloud hovering over my head wherever in the world I traveled. Yet I walked out from under that cloud and eventually began to feel better about myself. How did I do it? What steps did I take that I can chart for others to follow? How did I gain the faith in myself that I had never really had before? How did I learn to trust in others?

I think it was a gradual awakening to the reality of living. I began to understand that what I had been taught to believe did not and could not work. I believed, for example, that a woman should marry a man who could support her forever after. So even though I had a college education and had worked for years as a recreational social worker, I next married a man because he had a bright future and seemed like a good prospect. He was an army officer (captain) at the time. We got along like the calico cat and the gingham dog— scrapping continually, distrusting each other, criticizing. Yet I stayed in that impossible relationship for five years of mutual hell. I tried to be what I believed a "good wife" should be—another role. I tried to support him as a good wife should. All I succeeded in doing was undermining him, putting myself down, and feeling miserable. Why? Because I was trying hard to act a role that I believed in on an intellectual level but did not feel right in living.

I believed a woman should not compete in certain male-dominated types of employment. It simply did not occur to me to investigate engineering or dentistry or law for job opportunities. I even doubted that a woman should get a higher degree because she (I) would probably waste it. I remember a man saying to me once, "Why get a Ph.D.?—You don't need a degree to have babies." I felt angry at the time yet a little apprehensive. Although I was in graduate school, I secretly agreed; I was getting the education for my own pleasure. I believed that my husband would provide the support while I pursued my lifework—raising a family. So I went on to get an M.A. in English, believing that when I had children I would stay home with them, perhaps going into teaching later on. Any plans of mine, outside of my family, were decidedly secondary.

I rapidly let go of my former beliefs when I decided to leave my husband. I realized that I had not felt good for a full day at a time during the five years I had been married. I was continually so angry I began to think that if I stayed longer I would kill either him or myself. There were times I thought I had gone crazy. I did not know the person I had become. None of this made real sense to me then. I remember saying to my husband in an attempt to explain my reasons, "Feelings are more important than facts." The fact was that on the surface the marriage was progressing well, looked solid, and had real potential. My feelings were anger and frustration and discouragement. I did not really love my husband nor did I like living with him. I loved only my fantasy of him. Now I know that it was that fantasy which confused me. I doubt that I ever saw him as he really was: I visualized him only as I wanted him to be. When he did not act the way I thought he should, I was continually disappointed. Had I trusted my feelings, I would never have married him. And when I finally did act on my feelings, five years had passed me by.

After my divorce I enrolled in a doctoral program in drama, intending to write plays. After a switch in the administration of the drama department, I was informed that I had to write a critical dissertation instead. I soon became bored. One day I read a newspaper article about the work Dr. Cornelius Bakker (who later wrote *No Trespassing*) was doing in drama therapy. Drama therapy intrigued me, so I volunteered to work with Bakker and his staff. During several months of work with his Adult Development Program my entire direction changed. I learned that drama could be used to help people learn new and more appropriate ways of behaving.

By far the most important discovery I made at Bakker's clinic was that I, or anyone, could indeed change. Prior to that experience I believed that a person who had an unhappy childhood might go to a psychiatrist for years and years, yet remain unhappy. Who could afford years of treatment? And why bother if nothing changed? When I left that clinic I was a believer. I knew then that change was possible and available to everyone. I knew it could be achieved in a fairly short time for very little expense. As a start I needed to change my belief system. My life would change as a result.

I broke my habit of fantasizing by learning to stay in the here and now. I used to daydream a lot. My head was filled with escape routes out of my daily life. I was not aware of most of what went on around me because I was in some other world. I not only did not see other people, I did not hear them. I was so busy worrying about the future and kicking myself about the past that I had little awareness of Now. Gradually I began to understand that the moment and the place I am experiencing now is the only reality I can know in this life. I cannot guarantee the future, nor can I bring back the past. When I stay in the here and now, I expend my energy on being aware—of sounds, sights, tastes, smells, textures, feelings. I can enjoy living, without depressing myself or feeling anxious. And I can relate to people as they *are*, not as I think they should be.

Relating to others became a lot easier for me when I disposed of another erroneous belief—that the world revolved around me and everyone in it focused on me. When I walked into a room and people turned to look at me I assumed (another fantasy) that they were busily criticizing my not-okay self. Now I know otherwise. I know that the world does not center on me. I share its spotlight equally with millions. I know too that others view me as they view themselves. If other people pick me as the object of their criticism they undoubtedly criticize themselves severely as well. And that is their problem, not mine.

Once I changed this belief I was able to see people as they exist in the here and now. I no longer viewed them with suspicion, fearing their opinions of me. I began to like people more and more as I began to like myself. The less afraid I became, the more I could tolerate the behavior of others. Now I can drop my expectations of how they *should* act and deal with how they *do* act. And the less I expect them to act as I believe they *should*, the less angry and critical I become.

I have changed from an idealist and a romanticist into a realist. I no longer believe that other people should live up to my expectations. Nor do I believe that I should behave, think, and feel in ways that others expect. I accept my current feelings, thoughts, and behavior as parts of me. If what I say and do are accepted by others, that's great. If they do not accept me—tough!

I remarried a man who had as few expectations of me as I had of him. We had a baby girl when I was thirty-nine. I admit I had a few expectations of her, out of ignorance. I thought *having* the baby was the hardest part! I soon learned that *raising* her was tougher!

I no longer try to be a "good wife"; actually I have no idea of what that is. If I do not have time to cook, I ask him to do it. I often do not have time to do the dishes; recently he has been doing them more than I. Fortunately both my husband and I believe that household tasks need to be shared. We also believe that we are both capable of doing all kinds of work. He can do more than I can because he is stronger, but there are certain things he will not do, like iron or sort clothes. And I can do some things he cannot because my physiology is different and my hands are smaller, but there are things I will not do, like mow the lawn or take out the garbage. At times one of us may feel put upon, but it usually does not last because we express it. We do not have a perfect marriage because neither one of us is perfect. But it is very satisfying at times, sometimes fun and sometimes a drag, sometimes happy and sometimes a bore. And each of us feels it is okay to be who we are without being expected to be more or less; what else is there?

Nor do I try to be a "good mother." I soon found out that I did not like staying home every day with my little girl. When she was an infant, I was too tired to do anything other than stay home. I felt exhausted, trapped, and resentful much of the time. Somehow all the advertised pleasures of the homemaker did not alleviate my negative feelings. I got no pleasure out of waxing my floors (I remember being so tired my husband had to vacuum the floors for a year) or having the shiniest windows. Housework has always seemed so futile to me. I do not get jollies from baking; I know that if I bake it I eat it and then I get fat, so why bother? I do not knit or crochet or watch soap operas. I do like outdoor sports, travelling, and oil painting—none of which I was able to do when my child was a baby. When my daughter was about two-and-a-half years old, I remember spending many hours washing the walls with a sponge mop to work out my frustrations on something inanimate. I knew then as I know now that I will never be satisfied while staying home with no outside interest.

So I do not try to be a "good mother" and devote my life to my child. I do enjoy doing things with her. We go to movies and plays, to the zoo and to fairs. We go boating in summer and skiing in winter. We play games together and if I bake at all it is because she likes to do it. But I have my own life as does she. I teach and do therapy; she goes to school. We enjoy each other when we are together. When we get bored with each other, we are able to pursue our separate lives.

We also allow each other to express feelings verbally. When our daughter gets angry with either me or my husband she tells us, "I'm angry at you, mommy (or daddy)," even, "I hate you!" (What is hate but a very large anger?) We do *not* allow name calling, accusations, or physical violence. We are a permitting family, *not* a permissive one. Any verbal expression of feelings is okay within limits. When the verbal expression gets too loud I tell her to finish crying in her room because my ears are hurting. And usually after our daughter has told us about her anger she will give us a big hug along with, "I love you."

I remember one time when she smeared lipstick all over her face and the mirror. As I wiped it off she howled, "Mommy, I don't like you." I replied, "Honey, you don't have to like me." She thought for a moment, and then said, "Mommy, I really like you. I just don't like you now!"

She has permission to tell us about what she is feeling when she is feeling it. We have talked about feelings when we were not angry at each other, and she has confirmed what I have told her. She has asked me, "Mommy, when you are angry with me, do you still love me?" I have assured her that I do still love her and that I only stay angry at her for a little while. So she is able to accept my expression of feelings, and much of the time she changes her behavior. Once while we were waiting in a long checkout line at the grocery store she was whining and pulling at my coat because I refused to buy her some candy. I was getting uptight. I told her, "I'm getting very irritated at you for the way you're acting and I want you to stop." She stopped.

I have found that it is not easy to raise a child who is permitted to express her feelings. Sometimes I've caught myself wishing she did not express so many—or so loudly. Still, by sharing her feelings with child-like honesty, she has given me some of my deepest insights. One morning she was in a bad mood, tired from staying up too late the night before. She was crying, whining, and screaming.

Finally I said in exasperation, "I know you're tired and you don't feel good, but why are you taking it out on me?"

She threw her little head back and howled at the ceiling, "Because I don't have anybody else to take it out on!"

When I told my husband what she had said, we agreed that she was right. We do not allow her to mistreat the dogs. She is not permitted to act out at school. She has no brothers or sisters to fight with. She has no one else to take her bad feelings out on, except mom and dad. And if I don't try to be "good" why should I expect it of her?

I have not only stopped trying to be a "good" wife and mother, I do not even attempt to be a "nice" person anymore. I have discovered that being "nice" is a trap. I remember years ago when I would feel angry and show it, a voice in my head would say "Nice girls don't act that way." I would mentally whip myself for days or weeks until I managed to depress myself. Now I seldom whip myself. When I am angry I permit myself to express it. I went through a phase of believing that I was rotten when I got angry. I would have to tell myself "I'm okay even though I got angry." Now I no longer have to console myself. I simply believe it is okay to express anger directly and verbally. So I do not limit my behavior with the "nice" label. Sometimes I am warm and friendly and outgoing; other times I am cold and angry and withdrawn.

I have the feeling now that I am "real" most of the time, rather than the "nice" plastic caricature of a person I was in years past. I was such a nice, adaptive child. I tried so hard I naturally displeased others. I remember that when I was eight years old I went to a new school. The teacher, in an attempt to spread her favors, gave me a nickel and asked me to go to the lunchroom and get a carton of milk. It did not register with me that she wanted to drink the milk. I dutifully went to the lunchroom, bought the milk, and drank it myself. I felt humiliated when I realized that she had wanted the milk

for herself. For years afterwards I experienced feelings of humilia-
tion whenever I thought about the incident. I was so very, very
nice!

I feel far more comfortable now. I think other people feel more
at ease with me too. When I was nice, others did not really know
me. I did not dare let them know me because I was afraid they could
not possibly like me if they saw what was underneath the nice
exterior. Consequently people felt I was cold and distant. They
were right—I was. Now that I am no longer nice I feel comfortable
letting people know me as I really am. If they do not like me that is
okay too. I don't expect everyone in the whole world to like me. To
those who do not I say "That's your problem. You have missed
knowing a neat person."

I am still much the same person I was before I started to
change my attitudes. I do not deliberately hurt people because I
have stopped thinking of myself as nice, nor do I blow myself up to
put other people down. On the contrary, I think more highly of
other people because I think more highly of myself. I give others
more options to feel because I do the same for myself. I am aware
that when I criticize others, whether or not I verbalize my criticism,
I am also criticizing myself. Conversely, when I allow others to exist
as they are in the here and now, then I am allowing myself to *be* as
well.

I realize that in many other ways I am really the same person I
was before. Despite my good feelings and good days, I still have bad
days. They just do not occur as frequently, nor do they last as long.
I feel angry, hurt, scared, lonely, and sad at times, but now I feel
happy feelings more of the time. The difference now is that I accept
the bad feelings along with the good ones. I accept myself for what I
am rather than for what I *should be*.

I also accept the way I was as a child, understanding that my
feelings as a little kid were okay too. It was very appropriate for me
to feel lonely and small and afraid when I was little. I was small in
proportion to the big people around me. I was afraid because I could
not comprehend what was going on around me. Actually, I was right
on to feel lonely and small and afraid; any other feelings would have
meant that I was not in touch with the reality I was experiencing. I
was also smart to act nice, hold my angry feelings in, and behave
like a miniature adult. That is the behavior pattern my parents and

society expected of me. I must have been smart and right on; I managed to survive my childhood!

Now that I am a "big person" with a child of my own I understand that I no longer need those childhood feelings or behavior patterns. I no longer need to feel small or helpless because I am not small anymore and I am capable of helping myself. I do not need to feel afraid unless there is something in the here and now to fear. Of course, there are still times when I do have those childhood feelings. I think perhaps that I always will, albeit in diminishing amounts, because I am not now and never will be perfect. But now when I feel my archaic childhood feelings I can usually dispel them quickly by saying, "I am okay, I am okay, I am okay—whatever I am feeling and thinking." Excuse the repetition, but repetition helps stick it in my brain. Sometimes when I am feeling shaky I have to repeat, "I'm okay" a dozen times before it sticks! Or, "I am, therefore I'm worthwhile." I do not have to do anything or be anybody or have anything to prove I am worthwhile. I am worthwhile, okay, and perfect within myself because I exist—because I have survived!

Now I allow myself to feel whichever way I am feeling in regard to what is happening in the world around me, and I give others the same right. When I was little I had very limited options. My parents, my society, did not permit me to feel angry or resentful or hateful or rebellious or silly, so I did not express those feelings. I buried them alive inside of me and carried them around for years. And because my angry, negative feelings acted like a cork, bottling up any positive feelings inside me, for years I felt scared and depressed and sad and sick and lonely and tired. These were not enjoyable feelings; I was miserable, aching inside much of the time. But the feelings were familiar, and I did not have permission to feel any other way. People told me I *should* be happy, but how could I feel happy when I was *de*pressing myself with *re*pressed anger? Nor did I know I could change. When I found out that I could, it was a revelation to me, then a lot of hard, sometimes scary work, then pure joy.

When I was feeling very not okay I remember a sense of actually being two people. Sometimes I had the feeling of looking down on myself, watching the way I behaved, and criticizing myself severely for not acting the "right" way. When my upper self came down on the other me too harshly, I actually got a stiff neck and an aching back from tensing myself against the criticism. As I began to feel more okay I began to integrate my two selves. Now I no longer have a critical me above myself. I have become whole in a very real sense.

If I can let go of the feelings that caused me so much misery, change myself, and begin to enjoy my life, so can you. You will have to increase your awareness and learn to use certain tools in order to change. You must be willing to work on changing your beliefs, attitudes, and behavior. But if you want to, you can do it. I do not promise that it will be easy. I do promise that it can be done. The change in yourself may take years of work or it may take one day. Some insights that I have gained have given me new ways of behaving and new options to feel immediately; I have struggled with others for years.

Many students in my classes have turned their lives around in six to ten weeks because of their insights and changes in behavior patterns. In a recent class, one woman who had been separated from her husband for three months became aware of what she had been doing to destroy her marriage, and she reunited with her husband in a constructive, intimate relationship. Another, wishing for years to divorce her alcoholic husband but not daring to do so, became aware that she had the power to make it on her own and got a divorce. In another class, one man felt unable to go out for interviews, fearing that he would be rejected. Before the class was over he had gotten not only interviews but a job. Another man, who had worked hard for years with considerable success, decided that life was made for something other than work. He wanted to have fun with his family while he still could. He retired at the young age of forty-five. All of these are success stories. All were realized in less than ten weeks.

These people made new decisions about their roles in life and their ability to change. Their new decisions took the place of the old, destructive decisions that they had made in childhood. Once they *re*decided, they discovered their power to change the roles they acted and their lives. I do not mean to imply that all childhood decisions are made with deliberate intellectual awareness. I view the decisions a child makes on how to live his life as an interior, even subconscious process which may continue for many years. The same parent usually repeats messages to the child in the same way over the years. During this span of time the child may decide that these messages are right and accept them. The child may decide that the messages are wrong and either rebel against them or ignore them completely. Such decisions may be acted on for the rest of a person's life, long after the information on which the decisions were based has any validity. Some decisions are made instantly, based on a single traumatic childhood (or even grown-up) incident. Some can be sharply remembered. But more commonly the messages behind the decisions are given subtly, even nonverbally, over a period of years until they and the subsequent decisions are woven into the fabric of the person's mind.

In order for you to change, the computer of your mind needs to be reprogrammed. You need new information on which to base your redecision. I want to share with you some information so that you can accomplish your change. I also want to share with you some of my life experiences, along with those of other people I have known who have changed. I know that you can make new decisions about how you live your life. I know that you can learn to act in a way more appropriate for the real You. Tools are available for change. You can have hope. We can all make it!

2

Your power of choice

We are what we believe.
Change your beliefs
and find your power.

Our American heritage teaches that we can achieve anything we want to achieve and be anything we want to be. Millions of people have immigrated to our country in the hope that they could improve their status. By desire and willpower and a lot of hard work, millions have done it. In the 1800s, etiquette books were published by the dozens, preaching that anyone could rise to a position of respectability.* Books extolling the power of the individual are still rolling off the presses with great regularity, including this one. But this belief in each person's power of choice is viewed in different ways by different people.

One way was voiced to me by a woman in one of my classes. She said her mother had read and reread Norman Vincent Peale's *The Power of Positive Thinking*, "and ever since then she's been impossible to talk to. It can be raining buckets outside and she'll swear it's a beautiful day. And if I tell her I'm feeling bad she'll say, 'Now, now dear; just believe you're feeling good and you will be!' I

---

*Russel Lynes, *The Domesticated Americans* (New York, Harper & Row, 1963), p. 28

can't stand to be around her anymore." Many people have interpreted the power of choice in this way. They use it to sell themselves and others a fantasy trip. They ride their own high-flying bubble of pseudohappiness, refusing to acknowledge anything negative. Sooner or later the bubble bursts and they come down. Then they may kick themselves because they cannot stay on top. Once they have come down, the salesman's approach cannot quiet that tiny inner voice that says, "But I'm still feeling bad!"

Another way to view the power of choice is to believe everyone else has it. Everyone else in the whole world feels okay but you feel unique in your impotence—worthless, unimportant, and unable to change. The stronger your belief in your own lack of power, the more worthless you feel.

Such an attitude is exemplified by Marian T., a woman in her middle forties who came to me for therapy. She explained that she had been married for twenty years to a lawyer. She had worked as a secretary while he went to law school. She had raised their three children with little support from him. Because he was unable to get along with his supervisors, he changed locations every two or three years. Marian found it impossible to keep old friends and increasingly difficult to make new ones. Eventually she gave up trying. When her husband established his own practice he left her, telling her he could not live with a "bitch" like her any longer. He filed for divorce, and Marian decided to fight it to the best of her ability. She felt miserable and unable to cope. She had no friends, and even her children began to avoid her tears.

As she spoke of her depression Marian told me of her belief in her own uniqueness. "Nobody has a husband as unfair as mine," she said. "Nobody else feels as miserable as I do. And I can't do anything about it." Marian believed that her husband had all the power and that she had none. She blamed him for all her problems. She took no responsibility for her own part in the marital conflicts. By refusing to admit her own complicity in the conflicts Marian was actually giving away her power. She could not change him unless he was motivated to change, which he was not. And if she believed she was blameless she would not try to change her own behavior. She was truly powerless to change.

She also failed to see the difference between the realities of her situation and her beliefs about it. Marian believed that she felt certain emotions because of what happened to her. For instance, she assumed that she felt miserable because her husband treated her so badly. In schematic terms, she believed that **A** (her husband's actions) caused **E** (her emotions), or **A** → **E**. What she did not realize was that it was really her beliefs about her husband's actions (that he *should not* treat her badly) which influenced her feelings and caused her so much misery. A diagram of this relationship might appear **A** ⟋ **B** ⟍ **E**.* Emotions, though activated by actions, are greatly influenced by belief. The stronger the belief, the stronger the emotion will be.

When Marian became angry at her husband's criticism and put-downs, she responded appropriately to the situation; that is, she responded with her feelings to what was happening in the here and now. But when she continued to dwell on the incident, hold onto her anger, and escalate her emotion with her thoughts, she was responding inappropriately; that is, she was responding to her fantasies rather than to the actual event. Her anger, turned inwards, became long-term resentment and eventually depression. Certainly her husband had treated her badly, but it was Marian's own belief system that was continuing to make her so miserable.

When Marian was able to realize the strength of her beliefs about how her husband should act she could say, "Okay, so my husband treats me badly. That's the way he is now, the way he has always been, and probably the way he always will be. I can either accept his bad treatment and plead with him to take me back, or I can let the divorce go through. To tell the truth, I have acted like a bitch for most of our marriage because I don't like him. I don't want to live with him anymore and I won't go back to being the doormat I was before. The best I can do is negotiate through my lawyer for the best possible settlement." When Marian accepted the reality of her situation rather than holding onto her beliefs about it, she stopped saying, "Isn't it awful that he treats me so badly," and "I don't know what to do about it."

She also stopped putting the blame on her husband. She understood what she had been doing to keep the conflict going. In her

*Adapted from the book *A New Guide to Rational Living* by Albert Ellis, Ph.D. and Robert A. Harper, Ph.D. © 1975 by Institute for Rational Living, Inc. Published by Prentice-Hall, Inc., Englewood Cliffs, New Jersey.

case it was not only what she was doing but what she was not doing. She was accepting his bad treatment of her and she was not doing or saying anything about it. She began to understand that it takes two people to form an interaction. If two people are involved in a conflict, one person cannot put the blame solely on the other. A relationship can be compared to two hands clapping. Each hand is involved in the activity. One hand alone cannot clap anymore than one person alone can be fully responsible for a conflict within a relationship.

Marian's depression lifted when she became aware of her destructive belief system and decided to let those "shoulds" and "should nots" go. She chose to feel her anger towards her husband and express it. When he refused to communicate with her about their problems she decided to quit fighting and let the divorce go through. She got a well-paying job as an executive secretary and began feeling better than she had in years. She reestablished her relationship with her children and began to make new friends. She did not do all this overnight. Even today her metamorphosis is not complete. But she is able to relate more to people in the here and now and has stopped blaming her ex-husband for her problems. She knows now that she has as much power as anyone else in this world.

Some people believe that they have the power to achieve almost anything in the world. They rise above seemingly unconquerable odds. They apply almost superhuman effort and they achieve their goals. They become wealthy or powerful or famous. Then they find themselves still dissatisfied, searching for something they cannot describe. Bruce T. was one such person. An admittedly self-made man, semi-retired owner of an apartment complex at the age of thirty-eight, Bruce was still unhappy.

"I came to your class because I thought it might help me with this problem," he told me. "I've got everything a man could want—a great wife and kids, all the money and leisure time I need, everything I've ever asked for, but I still feel driven. Right now I'm negotiating a deal to mortgage my apartment and start in all over again. Then I asked myself, Why? What good would it accomplish? More money? I've got enough now. More leisure? I don't know what to do with myself half the time now. Besides, even with more of everything I'd still feel like I've got a monkey on my back."

His feeling of being driven was not the only problem Bruce

had. His power of choice allowed him to be a superachiever for his wife and children, but did not allow him to stand up for himself.

"I can't say 'no,' " Bruce confessed. "Whenever someone asks something of me I feel compelled to say 'Yes.' The only way I can wiggle out of it is to use my family as an alibi. I can stand up for them. But not for myself. Even if someone puts me down, I can't get mad at him. I usually end up finding excuses for him and blaming myself for what *he* did. My wife really gets mad at me sometimes but I can't seem to change."

During the class Bruce decided to call off his business negotiations, hold onto what he already had, and explore his feeling of being driven. He began to understand some of the reasons for his inability to say "No." By the end of the class Bruce said that he was beginning to tell people "No" for the first time in his life. But he still would not allow himself to get angry. He made an appointment for a therapy session.

In our first session Bruce told an incredible tale of childhood deprivation, neglect, and abuse. His mother had abandoned him, not once but many times. He had been shuffled from relative to children's home, from children's home to foster home, and back again. He had rarely had enough to eat and never enough warm clothes in the wintertime. He had not even owned a toothbrush until he was in high school. His life had been threatened routinely by one of his mother's boyfriends, and he had been beaten regularly by others. But no matter how many times his mother left him or foisted him off onto others, he always wanted to go back to her. Indeed, the more he endured for her sake, the more desperately he hoped that she would take him back with her and give him the love he craved. He cried for two hours that first session. I cried right along with him. It was one of the worst stories of parental neglect that I have ever heard.

"My mother left my father when I was four years old," he said. "She left my three older brothers behind one night and ran off with this drunk. At first I felt privileged that she took me along with her. But it was so rough. She had two sons by him. Then she started shacking up with other guys and she'd leave me to watch these kids. There'd be nothing in the house for me to feed them and this drunk would be waving his knife around swearing he'd kill us all and I wouldn't know what to do. Sometimes she wouldn't come back for days."

"How old were the boys when this was going on?" I asked.

"Oh, they were just babies," he said. "One, two years old. And mother told me I had to protect these kids. She'd say, 'Be a good boy, Brucie, and take care of your brothers.' But who was going to take care of me? She never took care of me; I was supposed to sympathize with her and chop wood for her and take care of her problems. When I'd try to tell her my problems she'd tell me I was a big boy and not to bother her. I was only five years old. And I was scared all the time."

"What did you feel when your mother left you, besides being scared. Did you ever get mad at her?" I asked.

"No, never," he said. "I still can't get mad at her. I guess I felt sorry for her. We were all in the same boat. We were all trapped in that town with that rotten madman. Finally, after he beat her up once too often we ran away. We hitched a ride on a truck going out of town and left. We had no money and she had no place to go so eventually the police picked us up. We kids ended up in the local detention center; I don't know where she was taken. I begged the authorities to let me take care of the babies; well, they were two and three by then. The police were kind. They let me keep the little one for the night. Then they took them both away."

He broke into uncontrollable sobs. When he finished crying I asked, "What happened to them?"

"I don't know," he said. "I never saw them again. I guess the state found foster homes for them. They knew my mother couldn't take care of any of us. My other brothers had all been placed in foster homes by that time. The babies must have been adopted later on because we never heard about them after that. My mother has asked about them from time to time but she never really tried to get them back. She has never taken care of any of us in her whole life!"

Bruce started to cry again. "She never tried to get me out of the detention home either," he sobbed. "I had to stay there for over a year. My brothers had it good; they were with families but I was in with all the robbers and tough guys. And I never knew why! I didn't do anything to deserve that!"

Bruce told me that when he was almost nine he was transferred to a children's home where there were no bars on the windows. He was given new clothes and enough food to eat, good food for a change. He could not understand why some boys wanted to run away.

"We even went to public school in town," he said. "That's the first time since first grade I was in a regular school. I liked it at first. But I was having a lot of trouble spelling. The teacher would give us tests and then put the papers up on the board. I couldn't understand how the other kids could get grades of ninety and one hundred and I was getting thirty or forty. The teacher finally told me I'd just have to study harder. So I studied. I studied until I knew those words backwards and forwards. When the teacher gave us the next test I went right through it. I was so proud. For the first time in my life I knew I had done something right and I felt like I could do anything in the whole world."

He started to cry again. "Then when I turned in my paper—that jerk of a teacher—I got every word right—100 percent—and that dummy accused me of copying another kid's paper. She gave me an "F." She wouldn't believe me that I spelled them all right. And I couldn't stand up for myself. I just shut up and took it."

Bruce told me of many more instances when he had tried hard to do what he thought others wanted of him but discovered that no matter what he did, he could not please them.

"I never knew the rules," he said. "They kept changing the rules and no one would ever tell me what they were. Like the time we visited that drunk's family. We had dinner there and for once in my life I had enough to eat. I knew there was pie for dessert because I had seen it in the kitchen. So I waited at the table after I finished and the adults kept talking and talking and talking. Finally I asked to be excused. Then when they got around to serving the pie I asked for my piece and they said, 'Oh, no, you can't have any pie; you left the table.' And I didn't get any pie. I had tried so hard to be polite and behave myself and it still wasn't good enough. I didn't know the rules."

Nevertheless, Bruce kept trying hard to please other people. When he began to work he found some employers who appreciated his willingness to please. Others took advantage of him, giving him little pay for long hours. Bruce did not dare to complain. Eventually, through sheer will power and tremendously hard work, he began to make money. He followed the lead of one of his employers in buying a piece of property and waiting for its value to rise. Then he built his apartment complex and found, for the first time in his life, that he had enough money. But he was still unhappy. He could not allow himself to enjoy what he had earned by his years of hard work. He felt guilty about spending his own money.

"Even when it comes to buying clothes," he said, "I feel guilty. If my wife didn't buy clothes for me I'd go around in rags. And I've never taken a vacation. Somehow it hasn't seemed like I deserved it."

Slowly, through therapy, Bruce began to let go of his painful past. He began to understand that his feelings of worthlessness were linked to his having been discounted by his parents since birth. He had been made to feel so unimportant to his parents that he could not feel important to himself. He also realized that he could never allow himself to feel angry because such emotion had been extremely dangerous when he was a child. If he had expressed anger to his mother, he feared she would have left him for good. If he had expressed any emotion to his "stepfather" (he never knew if his mother married her lovers) he knew that he could have been killed.

"If my head were on the chopping block and an axe was falling," he told me "my stepfather might have chosen me over a carrot lying there. But if it had been a bottle of whiskey, there'd have been no contest. He'd have grabbed the whiskey and let the axe chop my head off. He just didn't care. And then he was always threatening to chop off my fingers or slit my throat or shoot me. One night he got drunk and started shooting his gun off. He was angry at my mother but she wasn't there so he shot at me. He chased me all over the neighborhood. The only reason I got away was because it was dark. He'd have killed me. And he wouldn't have cared."

Bruce realized during therapy that he was still feeling sorry for his mother, just as he had when he was a child. No matter how she acted towards him, he could not feel angry at her; he usually blamed himself for not trying hard enough to please her. Slowly Bruce began to accept my permission that it was okay for him to get mad. And slowly he began to allow himself to express his anger. At first he only dared to get angry at strangers—a clerk in a department store, a waitress, or an erratic driver. He discovered that the world did not fall apart. For the most part they understood. One clerk even told him, "Yeah, I don't blame you; I'd be mad too at the treatment you're getting!" Then one day he experienced the feeling of anger towards his mother that he had never before allowed himself to feel.

"She used me," he said afterwards. "She would be out screwing around and she used me to do her work and babysit her kids. She didn't even know how that drunk treated me; she was always gone and I had to stay there and take his shit. She never believed me when I tried to tell her about him, either. She would just say, 'Now, Brucie, be a good boy and he won't hurt you.' And I would; I'd try harder to be good, always in the hope of getting her love. I'm still doing that. No matter what she wants she knows she can always call for Brucie because I'll break my back to do whatever she wants. Now, after all these years, I know it's useless. I can't get the love I want from her because she can't give it to me. She can't give anybody love. She's incapable of loving."

As he experienced this feeling his tears poured out amid sobs of anguish.

"I'm angry with her for all the years that she's destroyed for me," he continued. "But even more I'm sad; I'm sad for the little boy who fell for that bullshit all those years and tried to be so good in order to win her love."

"It's time you feel sad for that little boy," I said. "It's time you start taking care of him."

"Yes," he said. "I know now she will never take care of me. I know now that if I don't take care of myself nobody else will. Suddenly I feel empty inside. I'm filled with emptiness and it's a good feeling. I don't have to try to get her love anymore. And I don't have to be so damned good. I can just be me and if she doesn't like it, or if anybody else doesn't like it, damnit that's tough!"

"Right on!" I shouted, applauding his new awareness.

Bruce lost no time in acting on his feelings. He told his mother he would continue to offer her some financial support, as he had been doing for years, but that he would no longer be at her beck and call. He would not drive her to the grocery store or the hairdresser's or church when she snapped her fingers. He told her that she was perfectly capable of taking a bus or calling one of her neighbors. He no longer felt that he had to please her.

As Bruce got in contact with his long-buried anger and sadness he began to see changes in himself. For the first time in his life he began to really enjoy playing with his children. He felt more relaxed about seeing people and began to suggest to his wife, much to her surprise, that they do more visiting. He found that his voice had lowered; some of his friends had even commented that he no longer sounded like a pleading little boy. Most important to him, he began to experience a feeling of contentment that he had never felt before.

"I never realized I was that unhappy," he admitted. "It came out in such subtle ways. Like being so jealous of my wife that I panicked if she even wanted to go out with the girls. Or, like working twenty hours a day, seven days a week and convincing myself that I was doing it for the good of the family—all the while my family was begging me to spend more time with them. Now I understand that I've felt scared and panicky for most of my life and the only way I stayed one jump ahead of those feelings was by working my ass off for others! I never took time to have any fun. Everything I did was aimed at some vague future. I told my wife that when we got this we'd take a vacation, or when we got that we'd relax and enjoy life. But that time never seemed to come. I've lived in the future for years. Now, suddenly, I'm in the present. I'm right here and I'm enjoying being here. For the first time in my life I'm thinking about *me* and about how I can make my life more enjoyable. And somehow, I think my family's going to start having more fun too."

Bruce's power of choice had enabled him to set a goal and strive for it with all his might. It had not allowed him to enjoy his life along the path to that goal, or even to enjoy his achievement. When one goal was achieved, he immediately established another goal and started driving again. He was living in the future. Now he realized that he had to live in the future in order to obliterate the pain of his past. And he is beginning to be able to enjoy the Now.

The power of choice does not alter the past, nor does it guarantee the future. Certainly you can choose to drive toward the future with your power or you may use it to clutch tightly to your past. You can also use it to give yourself freedom in the present—freedom to relax, freedom to enjoy, freedom to be. To use your power of choice most effectively you need to stay in the here and now as much as you can. That means becoming aware of your fantasies, for when you are fantasizing you are not in the Now. You are in your head, spinning your mental wheels and wasting your energy. You are not perceiving what is happening around you, nor are you perceiving the people about you. You are blind to the Now. You are, like Oedipus, blindest when you have eyes to see.

When Oedipus had his sight he was closed off mentally from perceiving the truth. Sighted, he blocked awareness by intellectual fantasizing. When he lost his eyesight he also lost his inner blindness. He became able to perceive fully and developed more insight than when he could actually see. He learned, as you can, to open his inner sight to the truth, to reality. His perception enabled him to rightly comprehend the here and now through his remaining senses rather than his intellectual delusions.

Sandra S. was rarely in the Now when she came into my therapy group. She lived in the past and the future most of her waking hours. She also fantasized about people in the present. She had the common belief that she could read other people's minds.

One night Sandra told the group, "I like to dance but everytime I get out on the dance floor I know everyone is looking at me and saying, 'She can't dance, what's she doing up there?' or, 'Look at that ugly dress she's wearing; it's all out of style.' or, 'Did you ever see anybody as awkward on the dance floor as Sandra?' So I don't dance unless I drink so much I don't care what they say."

Sandra was fantasizing in a negative way, that is, she was hearing critical voices in her head. (Positive fantasy, on the other hand, can be very constructive.) The more Sandra fantasized about what people were thinking, the less inclined she was to expose herself to what she thought they were saying about her. The result was that she danced much less than she really wanted to. When she would get up to dance she ignored complimentary glances, believing that they were put-downs.

Like Sandra, Jeanne M. was fantasizing negatively when she came to see me. Jeanne believed that other people could read her mind. Jeanne believed that her husband knew what she wanted for her birthday and other special days. She believed he knew that she wanted surprise gifts, such as flowers or candy, at times for no reason at all. She also believed that he knew where she wanted to go if they went out to dinner. When he did not bring her what she wanted or take her where she wanted to go, she pouted. She believed he was deliberately being mean to her. Then, instead of telling him why she was angry she would give him the "silent treatment," sometimes for days. The fact that throughout thirty years of marriage, her husband had never been able to read her mind and give her what she wanted did not stop Jeanne from fantasizing that he should do so.

I believe it is humanly impossible to read another person's mind perfectly. You may have a good hunch about what a person is thinking or feeling. You can never be sure, however, until you check it out with that person. Even if you have extraordinary telepathic powers you cannot be sure your hunch is right unless you verify it. So I asked both Sandra and Jeanne to verbally communicate their fantasies to others in order to test their validity.

"What? Ask those people if they think I'm awkward?" Sandra bristled. "That's ridiculous! They'd think I was crazy!"

"I know it sounds ridiculous," I agreed, "but it's the only way you can find out what those other people are really thinking. You're fantasizing when you think that others are telling each other you're awkward. And you're still fantasizing when you say they'd think you were crazy if you asked. How do you know?"

"Well," Sandra said, "I guess you're right."

With that Sandra's belief system started to crumble. Later on she told me that she did check out some of her fantasies with other people. She was surprised to find out that they were usually looking at her in admiration. Some, of course, were looking at her because they had no one else to look at, with no judgment of her in their minds at all. But most of the people she asked complimented her on her dancing, on her outfits, and on her looks. Sandra started to feel a good deal better about herself. She even began to enjoy dancing without drinking first.

Jeanne too was surprised when she began to communicate her fantasies to her husband. She discovered that most of the time he had had no idea what she wanted, even though her hints were perfectly clear to her. When she began to tell him directly what gift she wanted or to which place she wanted to go, he felt relieved. He had often known that she expected something but he did not know what. He had feared displeasing her so he had done nothing. He had been bewildered by her prolonged silences because he had had no clear idea of why she was angry. Now he no longer felt pressured to guess what she wanted.

When Jeanne began to communicate her wishes to her husband, she began to get what she wanted for the first time in her life. She still had some reservations about stating her wishes openly, however.

"When I tell him what I want it doesn't seem as meaningful as if he would think of it himself," she confided. "But I am getting the presents I want. And he is taking me to some great restaurants for a change. I guess it's worth it!"

"How else are you going to get what you want unless you come right out and say it?" I said. "It's *okay* to ask for what you want!"

Jeanne began finding my permission message increasingly easier to accept. She had not been taught that by her parents. Like so many other people she had been taught that it was not polite to ask for what she wanted. "Don't ask, dear," were the words she heard, "wait until it is offered to you." Jeanne remembered other messages: "Don't be a pig; wait your turn," "Ladies don't act like that," and "Don't beg; it's not nice." Like so many other American women Jeanne had been taught to wait until a man made the suggestion. She had been taught that if she asked first he would think her forward, cheap, aggressive, pushy, masculine, crude, or not nice. So Jeanne had difficulty turning off those messages and substituting mine: "It is okay not to be nice!" The more she practiced turning off her "don't" messages, however, the easier it became for her. Both she and her husband discovered to their mutual delight that the "silent treatment" was a thing of the past thanks to their new ability to communicate.

Of course, being able to ask for what you want does not always mean that you will get it. So I added another permission message for Jeanne, "And if you ask for what you want, such as a bouquet of flowers, and your husband doesn't give it to you, go buy yourself a bouquet. You'll get what you want without wasting your energy on resentment and fantasies."

There are many words for fantasizing. It has many meanings in my dictionary: to assume, believe, worry, suppose, guess, take for granted, expect, foresee, rely, or deduce. And that is only a partial list. Pick the ones that you use. If you make a habit of this type of negative thinking you will find yourself feeling anxious over the future, depressed about the past, and confused about the present. You will find it difficult to concentrate, to remember clearly, to think logically, or to listen. You might scold yourself for not thinking enough when in actuality you are thinking too much. Your head is too filled with fantasizing to pay attention to the here and now.

I have had the experience many times of driving somewhere with the intention of turning at a certain road. Then, several miles after my turnoff point I will realize I missed it. "Miss No-Think," I used to say to myself. Now I say to myself, "Pay attention; you're thinking too much again."

I remember one night when I woke up in the early morning hours and started fantasizing about polar bears. There were two of them and they appeared out of nowhere. They were big, white, and very hungry. They were straight out of the Arctic wastes and they wanted food—me and my baby girl. So I spent the next hour mentally creating ladders to climb up, perches on top of the house to cling to while the bears paced hungrily below, and safe places to run to. I ran and climbed and agonized in my effort to escape the inexhaustible bears, until one rational thought finally invaded my fantasy. "What am I thinking about?" I asked myself. "There are no wild polar bears in Seattle!" So I got up and had some milk and cheese, knowing that I had wasted so much energy on my improbable fantasy that I would be dog-tired in the morning.

There is a difference between logical, constructive thinking that leads to the solution of a problem and "spinning your mental wheels round and round." There is a difference between positive fantasy in the form of constructive daydreaming, and visions of future calamity. There is a difference between planning rationally for the future and feeling anxious about it for improbable reasons, such as my polar bears. Anxiety is a rehearsal for a situation that will probably never happen. The more energy you expend rehearsing for the future, the less you will have to actually deal with it when the future becomes the here and now.

There is also a difference between remembering the past and depressing yourself over what might have been. "If only I hadn't quit my job" might lead to months of depression, months in which you might, more enjoyably and more constructively, have stayed in the here and now. If you depress yourself enough your body might slow down to the point of being nonfunctional. You may be unable to cook dinner, carry on a conversation, or read a book. Your physical functioning may be affected in more severe ways. You may feel nothing. You may become constipated. Your movements may become slow and lethargic. All this while your brain is buzzing away at the speed of a rocket out of control, wailing "If only . . ."

Anxiety and depression are not so much feelings as feeling-less states—ways to avoid feeling by listening to negative voices in your head and creating improbable fantasies to go along with them. Anything you do to increase your awareness of your intellectual fantasies may help you stop thinking and get you back into the here and now. Some people have good results from the behavior modification technique of counting the number of times they think self-defeating thoughts. They keep track of the numbers each day, checking to see how fast they can bring down the total. From thinking, "If only I hadn't moved," 100 times a day, your count may go down to only five times a day. I particularly like some of the methods that Ken Olson suggests in *The Art of Hanging Loose in an Uptight World.** If you find yourself fantasizing in the middle of the night, he says, get up and do some boring job until you are tired enough to turn off your mind. Explore your "what if" and "if only" tapes, as Olson calls them, by whatever method you can, and get in touch with the feelings behind them. Or give yourself permission to do whatever you fear might happen. You will probably find that your worst fears never materialize. I remember one client who was afraid she was going to throw up during a therapy session.

"Go ahead," I said. "The rug's seen worse than that with all the animals around here."

She took my permission and began to retch, continuing for about fifteen minutes. Finally she started to breathe easier, expressing amazement that she hadn't thrown up.

"I had faith," I said, "but if you had it would have been okay. But what would have happened if I had said, 'Don't throw up'," I asked.

"I'd have vomited all over the floor," she said firmly. So if you give yourself permission, there's no reason to try hard *not* to do whatever it is you're afraid of or, put it this way—permissions are great rug savers! I am aware that when I start to fantasize it's often

---

*Ken Olson, *The Art of Hanging Loose in an Uptight World* (Connecticut, Fawcett Books, 1974). Goes into "what if" and "if only" messages in detail.

because my body needs refueling. If I skip a meal, particularly breakfast, or eat only carbohydrates, I will often start not only to fantasize but to "calamitize"—feeling panicked by the vivid thoughts of death and destruction that fill my head. So I eat a protein snack to help myself back into the here and now. If you find yourself fantasizing regularly in a negative or destructive manner, be aware that your emotions and thoughts are greatly influenced by your dietary needs as well as by physical ailments. If you suspect that illness is the reason for your freaking out, take care of yourself by getting a physical checkup. It is much easier to stay in the here and now and feeling good about yourself when your body is fueled and healthy.

Aside from the physiological aspects, the primary reason you may be fantasizing is that you are listening to messages your parents gave you when you were very young, messages you still believe. One of the most debilitating of these, in my opinion, is the message that you can't do anything right. You may have been told when you got B's in school that you should have gotten A's, that you could have done whatever you did better, that you should always do your best, that you should do it right or not at all, that you should do it right the first time, and on and on and on. If you have been given these messages by your parents or parent figures loudly and often enough over the years, you may have come to believe that everything you do could have been done better; that it is not acceptable to make a mistake in anything; that no decision you make is really right; and that therefore there is no reason to try. If you do attempt anything, no matter how small, you might feel extremely anxious because you expect to fail. You may even "program" yourself for actual failure.

Barry W. was just starting out as a real estate agent when he came to see me. He was extremely discouraged because he was not selling any property, his finances were at an all-time low, and he was afraid he was going to be a complete failure. He told me that he had failed several times before in business and that he could not bear the thought of doing it again. Barry said his father had been a failure too and had committed suicide. He did not want to take the same route.

"So you're a perfectionist," I said.

"No, I'm not," he replied. "I'm a failure."

"Of course," I said. "You wouldn't be a perfectionist if you didn't believe you were a failure."

"I don't understand," Barry said.

Instead of wasting my breath with explanations, I asked Barry to do a Gestalt exercise to get in touch with the origins of his perfectionist feelings.

"Who told you most often," I asked him, "that you couldn't do anything right?"

"My mother and my grandmother," he said without hesitation.

I set the stage for a conversation between the three of them. As he talked to his imaginary mother and grandmother, Barry remembered how they had continually criticized him for what he did. The only attention he got from them was when he did something wrong.

"You're not doing that right," Barry said, role-playing his mother. "You never do anything right, you always screw up. Why can't you be like your brother? You're going to end up a no-good bum, just like your father." As his grandmother, Barry said, "You're a bad boy, Barry. You're like your father's side of the family, always in trouble. I told your mother not to marry him but she would have her way. And you've turned out just like him. Now you listen to me, boy. I know best. You do what I tell you and you'll get by. But follow your father's example and you'll never make it."

Barry began to understand that his mother and grandmother had programmed him for failure by telling him that he could not do anything right. They even set him up for suicide. When his father killed himself Barry saw the act as his own logical outcome, since he had been told so often over the years that he was "just like" his father. Through his work in therapy Barry was able to express his anger towards his mother and grandmother. He was able to separate himself from his father's image. He let go his sorrow over his father's death, suddenly comprehending the act as his father's tragedy and not his own. He also started allowing himself to succeed. He stopped scolding and criticizing himself harshly when he lost a sale. And he stopped kicking himself for making mistakes. As he changed, Barry became happier and more relaxed. He became an enthusiastic salesman and he started to make money. When I last heard from Barry, he was enjoying his work and was well on his way toward achieving financial success.

Doris C. also believed she was a failure. She had grown up a lonely only child, living with her parents on an isolated farm. She had had no exposure to other children until she was in the first grade, and no relatives nearby with whom to identify except her parents. Her parents never verbalized their feelings. Doris had always felt their anger was directed toward her even when she knew they were angry with each other.

Her parents gave her very strong messages, both verbally and nonverbally, that she was incapable of doing anything right. Her father criticized her continually with heavy sighs and harsh glances from an angry face that said to her, "You're to blame." Her mother had always presented an image of rigidity with the underlying nonverbal message, "Don't get too close." Doris's mother did not allow her to cook, sew, or clean the house. When Doris tried to learn these skills her mother became exasperated and did the work for her. This only added to her feelings of inadequacy and incompetence.

When Doris came to me for therapy she believed she had failed at marriage, at child-raising and at being a homemaker. She had been divorced for three years. Both of her children were seeing psychiatrists, as had she for several years. She wanted to get a job, but her belief that she would fail was so strong that she would not even go for an interview. She also agonized endlessly over mistakes she thought she made in whatever she said and did. She was tense, tired, and worried most of the time.

"Doris," I told her during one group meeting, "it is okay to make mistakes."

"Of course it is," she said, "for everyone else. But not for me."

"It is okay for you too," I said. "Not only little mistakes but the biggies too."

"Maybe I could accept doing some little thing wrong, like saying the wrong thing or wearing the wrong dress to a party or not responding the right way to someone," she said. "But I can't accept that about the big things. They're so—irrevocable. I can't take them back."

"You're right," I said. "You can't." And with that we got into decision making. One of Doris's big problems at this point in her life was not feeling able to make decisions. Because of her fantasies about never being right she believed that no matter which decision she made she would be wrong. So she made none. When I agreed that she could not go back and remake her decisions she felt even more uneasy. I also agreed with her that she might make the wrong decisions in the future.

"In fact," I told her, "no matter which choice you make, if you look at it in one way, you will make the wrong decision."

"Oh, great," Doris said. "That's all I need."

"But if you look at it the other way," I continued, "every decision you make will be right."

I explained my belief that every decision is like a fork in the road. Robert Frost's poem "The Road Not Taken" fits my concept of decision making precisely. Like a fork in the road, every decision can be made—or taken—in two ways. Each alternative has its good points and its bad points. Many opposing decisions are "really about the same." I have paused, like Frost's traveller, many a time at a fork in the road, not knowing which way to go, then moved on, not because I knew I was making the "right" decision, but because I knew I would grow roots if I stood there long enough. Few decisions are clearly "right" or "wrong."

I realized this with a jolt one day as I listened to a woman telling me about a decision she had made several years before. She had been offered a job abroad which she decided not to take, choosing instead to accept a marriage proposal. When she came to me she had a husband and three children, all of whom she loved, but she still regretted not having gone to Europe. She thought she had made the wrong decision by getting married.

"Wait a minute," I said. "I did just that! I went to Europe, even though I could have stayed in the States to marry and have a family—and I've always thought I made the wrong decision! I've kicked myself for having wasted all those years travelling and seeing Europe instead of building a life here, while you've kicked yourself for doing just the opposite."

I understood then that there is no such thing as a totally right or a totally wrong decision. Some decisions are better than others but each person will make some decisions that turn out badly. The one valid statement I can make is that each decision is different, like forks in a road, and each has different consequences. I had different experiences in my European travels than the woman who married and raised a family. We each experienced both positive and negative feelings on our different paths. Neither my decision nor hers had turned out entirely right or wrong.

I spoke earlier of the decisions a child makes as an interior process which takes place over a period of years. Certainly those interior decisions are made in a different manner than deliberate, intellectual decisions we make as adults, but that is not to say that we don't or shouldn't make interior decisions as adults. The interior decision seems to be based more on how we feel, while the rational decision is one that is made by thinking out a problem and deciding, intellectually, upon a solution. Either kind of decision, taken alone, can get us in the soup! The decision which may be the "best," if there is a best, is that which is based on both how we feel about the problem and on consideration of the available information. I know that if I make an intellectual decision without taking my feelings into account, I will most likely suffer later on. On the other hand I have made some very good intellectual decisions which I knew opposed what I felt. For example, I may have arranged to give a speech at a conference. When I enter the room I see a hundred people waiting to hear my speech. I feel scared. Based on my feelings, my decision would be to get out of there as fast as I can. But rationally, I decide to simply be aware of my terror and go ahead with the speech anyway. From a rational point of view, that decision would seem the most appropriate.

Whatever the basis for the decision, our saving grace is the fact that most decisions are not irreversible. Although a decision, once made and acted upon, is done and past, a totally different decision can usually be made in the future. As I explained to Doris, if you can accept both the "right" and the "wrong" parts of your decision, there is no reason to avoid making it. If you find that the wrong outweighs the right you can make a different decision later on.

"It's okay to change your mind," I told Doris.

"You mean that nothing is forever?" she asked.

"That's it," I said. "Life is change. If you can be aware of how you feel in regard to a continually changing environment, you can make your decisions, even if they may seem contradictory, so that they are most right for you."

"I see," she said. "I'll think about it. And," she added quickly, "stay aware of how I feel in regard to my environment."

"You've got it," I said.

The worst word in the English language, I have come to believe, is "should." Equally bad are such terms as "got to," "must," "have to," and "ought to," and all of their negative forms as well. When someone tells me a "should" or "should not" in one of its many forms, I react as if I have seen a cobra crawling through the grass. When I become aware of that "should snake" I know that whoever is using it is fantasizing. There is some expectation implicit in that person's mind that keeps that person from viewing reality as it is.

One exercise that is helpful in becoming aware of your "shoulds" is to make up sentences starting with "I have to." Make up several that have meaning for you. Next change the first three words of all these sentences to "I choose to." Now let's argue about it. You might say, "But I don't really choose to work or clean house or take of my kids—I have to!" My answer to this is although it may be true that you do not really want to take care of these obligations, you do have the power of choice. You could go on welfare or have a dirty house or let your kids run in the streets. You are choosing to do what you do because you do not want the alternatives. Now you might say, "So what good does that do me? Even if I'm choosing, I still have to do these things." Yes, you still do these things, but if you can understand your own responsibility in choosing, you will have no reason to resent those around you. Nobody makes you do what you do. You choose even if you do not particularly like the outcome of your choice. And in realizing that you are choosing, you may not change what you do, but you will change your attitude about it.

The next step in the exercise is to make up several sentences starting with "I can't." You might say, "I can't fly," or "I can't breathe underwater," or "I can't speak to large groups." Now change the first two words of your sentences to "I won't." Some of your sentences may really be "can'ts." You may truly be unable to fly as a bird does because you do not have wings. You may be unable to breathe underwater or live your life over again or win an Olympic medal at age fifty. But many of your "can'ts" are actually "won'ts." If you say, "I can't speak Spanish," I would say that you may not be able to speak it now, but you could take lessons and learn. If you say, "I can't speak to a large group of people," I would tell you to work through your fear by speaking to small groups first, then larger and larger ones. You might also take a speech class or, if your fear still hinders you, undergo therapy. If you can change your "can't" into "won't" you will be able to say "I will if I want to." You then have the power of choosing what you want to do or what you do not want to do. You release yourself from helpless "can'ts" and give yourself the power to change what you want to change and do what you want to do.

Self-limiting "can'ts" are often used to rebel indirectly against a "should." I struggled to sew for years and made clothes that did not fit, had crooked seams, and looked terrible. I rarely wore what I had sewn and usually hid it away in a closet. Still I struggled to sew, thinking, I realized later, "I *should* be able to sew." I suppose I was laboring under the cultural edict that all good wives should be able to sew, cook, and tend children. When I used this exercise I changed "I can't sew" to "I won't sew."

"Wow," I realized, "I don't want to sew! That's right, I won't sew because I don't like to sew!" With that awareness I felt the burden of "should" lift from my shoulders. I stopped struggling to sew and quit kicking myself mentally for not "being able" to sew. Of course I could sew if I really wanted to!

I became aware that when I used "can't," I felt helpless and frustrated; even my voice changed to a higher, whining pitch. I felt angry, too, but did not know who to blame. Now I know that my use of "can't" was a mechanism I employed to evade the parent messages in my head, the "shoulds." When I was a child, it was also a very handy device for getting attention and help. I no longer need that device. I know that I am able to make my own choices now. I can ask for help directly. If I do not want to do something I can come out of hiding and take responsibility for my choice by saying "I won't."

Some people feel compelled to outwardly rebel against "shoulds," rather than adapt to them. Sometimes these people find themselves not doing what they would really like to be doing because their habit of rebelling is too strong. They may hear hidden commands in words the rest of us accept as the most innocuous. I remember one evening, as a group was leaving my house, I said to Carol B., "Have a good week!" She returned, "I will if I want to!"

Carol had a strong compulsion to rebel, having had domineering parents who placed many expectations on her. They had also expected her to be angry and do the opposite of what they wanted her to do. With the group's help Carol worked out the following permission: "It's okay to do what you want to do even if someone else wants you to do it." When she started to believe that permission, Carol became more able to do what she chose to do, even if someone else gave her a command to do it first.

The "shoulds" in your head, which can also be called bias, prejudice, or expectations, are often well hidden. I have learned to listen carefully for them. Karen J. called me one day, very upset. She had had a disagreement with her ex-husband over their son. She told me that she had listened to his complaints over the phone for fifteen minutes about the way she was raising their boy. When she had tried to give her opinions he refused to listen. He had hung up on her.

"I was courteous enough to listen to him; why couldn't he do the same for me?" she asked.

"You mean, why shouldn't he," I said. "And why should you expect him to suddenly be courteous to you now, when you have said he was not courteous when you were married to him?"

"Well, why shouldn't he?" she replied. "After all, I've tried to be nice to him for our son's sake."

"That's why you're upsetting yourself," I said. "Because you are trying to be nice to him and keep the peace, you fantasize that he should do the same to you. Do you really believe, after being married to him for five years, that he wants to be nice to you now?"

"Well, no," she admitted. "He was nasty before and there's really no reason to expect him to be different now."

"Right," I said. "So, if he's not going to change, why expect him to act differently than he does? Accept the fact that he is acting badly and has as long as you have known him. Certainly you can express your anger to him, but instead of getting upset over his behavior, you can tell yourself, 'Okay, so he's behaving as usual. That's the way he is and no expectation of mine will ever change him.' Then, even though you're angry to begin with, you won't allow your expectations to escalate your anger. Once you express your anger and see the reality of the situation, rather than hang onto your 'shoulds' about it, you'll quit upsetting yourself."

"You're right," she said. "He is an s.o.b. and has been as long as I've known him. If he wouldn't treat me decently while we were married why should I expect him to change now? I'll just expect him to act the way he's always acted. Then I'll get along fine with him. When he says something mean I'll consider the source and let it go."

When Karen realized there was no logical reason why her ex-husband should be nice to her, she also became aware that she need not try to be nice to him anymore. She could drop that self-limiting role and deal with him according to her real feelings. Karen realized that she did not need to depend on his liking her to feel good about herself. She realized that if he did not express his affection during their married life together, there was no use worrying about his dislike now. So she decided to express her real feelings to him without concerning herself about his reaction. And she did feel better about herself, even when he reacted angrily to what she expressed. She called me up in exhilaration one day to report a conversation with him.

"I told him I was really mad at him for not listening to my opinion, and I didn't like his hanging up on me," she said. "He started to swear at me and call me names. I didn't cry like I usually do and I didn't defend myself. All I did was say to him, 'My, you really sound angry at what I just said.' And you know, he suddenly became nice and apologized to me. What do you know about that!"

Karen's power of choice enabled her to change her behavior, and in so doing, to change the behavior of her ex-husband. When she dropped the "shoulds" from her belief system, she allowed herself to view him as he really was in the here and now. He responded with less anger because she was not pressuring him to be what she thought he should be. I have no doubt that their marriage would have been considerably different if both she and her husband had seen each other as they really were. Few people are really malicious s.o.b.'s by intention. But many people act as if they are when they are weighted down by other people's "shoulds."

I find it hard enough to confront someone's "shoulds" when that person understands how destructive those beliefs are. When someone believes that his "shoulds" are absolutely right on an intellectual level, however, the process of letting the message go may take twice as long.

Natalie K., a woman in one of my groups who believed her

"shoulds" were right, declared one day, "I have the feeling that everything I do is wrong. Still, I have a feeling of self-righteousness because I tried to do what was right though it was never good enough. And I have an expectation too that because I tried, then the other person should do what I expect him to do. I've done my part, now he should do his. If I take responsibility for something, the other person should take responsibility too. And if he doesn't I resent him tremendously."

The issue of "right" vs. "wrong" that Natalie raised is one which I personally find very confusing. Certainly I can label some acts "wrong" without hesitation. Murder is wrong. Beatings are wrong. Malicious criticism is wrong. But what about killing in self-defense? Or an occasional swat on the bottom of a misbehaving child? Or satire? There are so many degrees of right and wrong. I prefer to eliminate my confusion by thinking all feelings are okay and all thoughts are okay, even though I may not agree with someone else's, but actions must be judged individually. And I do not expect my judgement of any act to necessarily agree with the opinion of anyone else.

Our problem with "shoulds" is that they are usually based on an acceptance of or rebellion against one's parents' standards—their rights and wrongs. Most of us were raised by parents who used a great deal of negative criticism to mold us into their ideal of model children (as they had been molded by their parents). So I learned more about what was wrong with me as a child than what was right. In fact, sometimes it seemed to me that what was right was anything I was *not* doing. You probably had similar experiences.

Since my "shoulds" have been set up for me by my parents and parent figures, they are not absolute. They are arbitrary, therefore they cannot be right. And, being arbitrary and of someone else's making, they cannot be right for me. What is right for me *feels* right for me. So I do not try, as Natalie does, to "do what is right" anymore. I do not want to be right or wrong, bad or good. I only want to be me. And in being me, I find my power.

In the same ways that I find and accept my power, you can find and accept yours. When you take responsibility for your feelings, thoughts, and actions, you begin to have the power to do what you want to do. You can then change your attitudes and your behavior. You may even find that as you change your family members begin to change too because you are no longer putting the blame on them and accusing them of "making you feel" one way or the other. As you own your feelings and give others the responsibility for theirs, you "unhook" from each other in an emotional sense. Your changing will free others to change if they so choose. Your children may start changing first because they're less set in their behavior patterns, and the oldest generations, probably last. Make up your mind now that it won't be easy. The first time your child says to you, "I'm mad at you, mommy (or daddy)," you may be tempted to reply, "Don't talk to your mother (or father) like that!" But hang in there, it gets easier!

Of course, others around you may choose not to change. Who wants to willingly suffer the upset of change? I sometimes think that the reason we change is that we are too frustrated by circumstances *not* to do so. Others around us may not feel the same frustrations. They may want to go along as they have before, even though life is less than satisfying. They may resist any change at all in a determined effort to hang onto the status quo. And if they are so determined to stay put, no change of ours, no nagging or persuading or making ultimatums will move them. That is simply where they are and where they have decided to be.

But you can go ahead and change, regardless of those around you. Even if they try to hook you back into your old familiar though miserable behavior patterns, you can do it. Change is not impossible; it only seems that way at times. If you are willing and motivated enough to persist in your quest for personal growth, you will realize your own power of choice, and with it your ability to change your life.

Survival through roles

The roots of our roles
grow out of a genuine need—
our very survival.

A popular misconception about Charles Darwin's theory of evolution is that the strongest of the species survive in the process of natural selection while the weakest perish. "Be strong and you will make it; be weak and you may not," many parents tell their children, believing strength will help them to survive in a hostile world. Actually, "strength" has less pertinence to the theory of evolution than the concept of "adaptation"—changes in form and behavior resulting in greater harmony with environmental conditions and better chances of survival. To "be strong" in the way we are taught by our parents does *not* help us to cooperate with others in our social environment but may threaten our survival or even cause our demise.

Certainly the survival of each species depends to some degree on the strength of its individual members. Most important, however, is the ability of those members to adapt to their environment. The study of evolution is the study of the continuing adaptive responses of all living things throughout the millenia. Even when conditions have remained fairly constant there has been some degree of adaptation necessary for survival. When the environment has changed drastically, many species have perished. We are all familiar with the story of the dinosaurs, creatures of immense strength who died out when climatic conditions changed. Such occurrences are commonplace in the history of evolution and have been rapidly increasing in frequency with the expansion of human civilization. Many animals have become extinct in our lifetime, and others are threatened yearly by the environmental impact of increased pollution and the spread of humanity. Strength alone will not save these species. If the present trend of environmental exploitation continues, few of them will adapt quickly enough to their changing environment to preserve themselves. Even the existence of our own species is threatened by these environmental changes. The question today becomes, "Can we maintain an environment hospitable to human and animal life and if not, do we have the ability to adapt to a poisonous earth?"

As each individual species must continue adapting in order to survive in its physical environment, so must each individual person adapt within the climate of a family to ensure physical and psychological survival. Adaptation in this sense does not involve physical changes such as those which enabled our distant ancestors to crawl out of the ocean or to stand on two legs. Adaptation is a less tangible process in the context of the family, though nonetheless real. By adapting to the desires of parents and siblings, infants learn which roles to play. Because of particular adaptations, most children are accepted by their families and allowed to remain within their confines. Children fear that if they do not adapt, their families might cast them out or withhold food and protection. When faced with the fear of abandonment, most infants choose to adapt and survive, no matter how self-destructive their adaptation may be.

Babies are born helpless and unable to meet their own needs; they must rely on their parents to care for them. If their parents give them food and shelter but do not accept them and love them, the infants will be emotionally, even physically, stunted. Some babies wither away because they do not have enough physical touching and emotional warmth, even though they have adequate food.* So babies learn very early in life to give their parents what they

---

*Eric Berne, *Transactional Analysis in Psychotherapy: A Systematic Individual and Social Psychiatry* (New York, Ballantine Books, Grove Press, 1961), p. 77.

want in order to be accepted and fulfill their own needs for nurturing. If parents demand hugs and kisses the infants may be affectionate; if parents demand anger they may learn hostility; if parents do not want to be bothered they may learn withdrawal. I say, they "may," because even babies have the power of choice in their responses to the demands placed upon them. They may adapt to those demands or rebel against them. While some babies adapt to indifference by withdrawing, others may insist on bothering their parents because they see negative attention as better than no attention at all. And if their parents respond by giving them spankings and scoldings, they may continue to demand that type of attention from those around for the rest of their lives.

So babies adapt in order to be accepted and in order to survive. They develop dependencies upon their parents to satisfy their needs, as their parents do upon them. This type of mutual dependency is called a "symbiosis." The original symbiosis, developed with the mother, is life-sustaining. When a baby cries, a mother's milk may begin to flow, an example of a symbiosis in its most basic form. Other symbioses may become more convoluted. If the dependency involves repeated negative messages, perhaps reinforced with physical punishment, the symbiotic bond will be destructive for the child and extremely difficult to sever. If a child has been told often enough, "You're stupid, you can't do anything right," reinforced with spankings the child may adapt by deciding, "Okay, mom, if you say so, that's what I am." The child may continue to prove the "You're stupid" message by getting poor grades in school, avoiding responsibility, and failing at all endeavors. Conversely the child may decide, "No, I'm not stupid and I'm going to prove it!" That child may go on to get a Ph.D., as I did to prove to myself how smart I was, even though I still heard the message in my own mind from time to time, "You're stupid."

Whatever the infant's original adaptations, or symbiosis, it is an appropriate one to his situation if the child survives. Even a destructive kind of symbiosis is constructive in that it sustains life. The problem with this survival mechanism is that it becomes so ingrained in the individual's personality that it may create problems later on. When such children grow up, instead of being able to relate to others as they are in the here and now, they may relate as they were in the there and then. That is, even though they may be thirty or forty or sixty years old, they still may be using the same adaptive responses they learned in their original symbiotic relationships during infancy.

At the first meeting of one of my classes, Lynn E. asked a great many questions. Before I could respond to a question she would invariably ask it two or three different ways. I felt irritated at this and told her so.

"I know I turn people off and offend them," she said. "People have told me this all my life."

"Do you think you will not be heard if you ask the question only once?" I asked.

"Oh, yes," she said. "No one ever listens to me. My mother has never listened to me. She still doesn't. She's too busy criticizing me to bother listening."

In her adaptation to her original symbiosis, Lynn had learned to demand a response by repeating her questions. Not expecting to be heard, she had tried overly hard to capture the attention of whomever she was with. When people became irritated with this behavior and responded with anger she had accepted their response as her due. Her mother had always responded in such a manner, so why shouldn't everyone else? Lynn was relating to others in the here and now as she had learned to relate to her mother when she was three years old.

The messages that children receive plus the decisions they make about them form images in their minds. They model their behavior on these images, constructing roles which they present to the world. Marv S. was reluctant to reveal the origin of his problem when he came to me for therapy. He told me he had difficulties relating to women, particularly during sexual encounters. He said that no matter how hard he tried, his sex life was a disaster. After much hesitation he told me of an experience he had as a child.

His father had been in the Army during the Korean War. Marv was five years old when his father returned from overseas, and he felt deep resentment for the tall stranger who intruded on his relationship with his mother. When his mother and father talked, he felt jealous and abandoned. One evening, after his father had been home for a few weeks, his mother was giving him a bath. Marv had always enjoyed having his mother bathe him. This time he had an erection. He does not remember his mother saying anything but he received a strong nonverbal message that she disapproved. She left him in the tub and went out to talk to his father. After awhile his father came in and finished bathing him. His father told him that he was big enough to start bathing himself. His mother never bathed him again. In his five-year-old mind Marv thought that he was to blame.

"I thought I was a bad boy," he said. "If only she had scolded me, even spanked me. But neither she nor my father ever spoke of it. Their silence was worse than anything else."

"Do you still think you're a bad boy?" I asked.

"I guess I do," he said. "A lot of times when I get an erection I feel bad, even guilty, and then—zap, there's nothing. My girl friend is about to call it quits."

"Fritz Perls has said," I told him, "that behind every guilt, there's resentment; behind every resentment, a demand.* Let's see if we can get you in touch with the resentment and demand behind your guilt."

Marv got in touch with his true feelings and found that he did indeed resent his mother. She had laid her own sexual hangups on him by her nonverbal disapproval. She did this, he discovered, in many subtle ways over the years. Marv found that his unmet demand had been for her to allow him to be a feeling child. He discovered that she had given him many, many messages throughout his childhood that he should not feel. And he realized that, as an adult, he was still turning off his feelings. Not only did he turn off his expression of anger, but also his excitement. When he turned off his feelings during a sexual encounter, the result was disastrous.

Marv also found that he resented his father for not protecting him from his mother. His unmet demand had been for his father to show him how to be a man by setting the right kind of example. Instead, his father had allowed Marv's mother to dictate how the boy was to be raised, without objecting. In fact, his father rarely expressed an opinion on anything. He allowed Marv's mother to make up all the rules. And he gave in to the mother's demands in every case.

"My father was a wimp," Marv said, "and that's just what I am.

*Frederick S. Perls, M.D., Ph.D., *Gestalt Therapy Verbatim* (New York, Bantam Books, Real People Press, 1974). See p. 51 for discussion.

I can't stand up for myself anymore than he could. I don't like him and I don't like myself."

Through therapy Marv was able to separate his self image from that of his father. He was able to start giving himself permission to feel and to have opinions. He was also able to see that his judgment of himself as a bad boy for having sexual feelings was no longer valid. It did not take him many sessions to realize that he could change that image and start accepting himself as a worthwhile human being, no matter what his feelings were. With a different self image he no longer worried about his sexual performance, as a result of which it improved immeasurably. And, he told me later, his relationship with his girl friend also improved.

So children learn from their parents' verbal and nonverbal messages about which roles they should play and how they should live their lives. Parents are responsible for transmitting behavior to their children. Yet parents are not to blame for their children's behavior for two reasons. First, the parents themselves learned their behavior from their own parents and taught their children only what they themselves had learned. How could they teach what they did not know? Second, every child can decide which message to adapt to, which to rebel against, and which to ignore. The child may not be aware of having chosen; nonetheless, that child did make some choice.

I believe that the great majority of parents want their children to have good lives, to be successful and happy, and live for a long time. They teach destructive messages and roles to their children not because of malicious intent but because they do not know any other way. And the old, tried and true, destructive ways have a history. I can understand the origins of some of our messages by examining their roots in American history. In the Puritan culture children were raised to be humble and self-effacing. These qualities were considered virtues. The natural tendency of a child to rebel, starting at about two years of age, was viewed as a tendency toward corruption. Any attempt to exhibit a mind of one's own on the part of the child was called "stubbornness" by the parents and was "broken and beaten down."* Children were expected to become miniature models of their parents and accede to their elders' wishes.

*John Demos, *A Little Commonwealth: Family Life in Plymouth Colony* (New York, Oxford University Press, 1970), p. 135.

They were not permitted to express their feelings. Anger in particular was regarded as evil; no circumstance could ever justify its expression.

Of course we can go farther back than Puritan times to view childhood in another perspective than that we know today. In a five-year study on child rearing practices throughout history, Lloyd DeMause found that the helping attitude that today's parents exhibit toward their children is a fairly recent trend. He says:

> A child's life prior to modern times was uniformly bleak. Virtually every child-rearing tract from antiquity to the 18th century recommended the beating of children. We found no examples from this period in which a child wasn't beaten, and hundreds of instances of not only beating, but battering, beginning in infancy.*

Other forms of child abuse were not only commom but accepted practice of disciplining children. Swaddling infants so that they were immobile was a common practice, as was sending the child of wealthy parents out to the homes of wet nurses for the first few years of life. Terrorizing children with stories of the Devil, ghosts, or the dead in order to make them behave was common. In England, DeMause goes on, "A common moral lesson involved taking children to visit the gibbet, where they were forced to inspect rotting corpses hanging there as an example of what happens to bad children when they grow up."† Sexual abuse, torture, and infanticide were all practiced by various cultures throughout the centuries.

People generally believed that children were like little animals, having to be disciplined or punished in order to become socialized. They also believed that children were not as important as adults, that they did not know what was good for them, and that they should behave at all times. These beliefs have not entirely disappeared. Even today I see families operating on these beliefs and experiencing problems because of them. Some of the messages I hear people giving their kids today include: "Children should be seen and not heard," "children should not fight among themselves," and "children should love their parents." Once I made the statement

---

*Lloyd DeMause, "Our Forebears Made Childhood a Nightmare," *Psychology Today* (April, 1975, V. 8, No. 11, Ziff-Davis Pub. Co., Boulder, Colo.), p. 85.

†DeMause, p. 86.

at a lecture, "It's okay for a child to express his anger to whomever he is angry at." One startled parent responded, "But not to me! I'm his mother!"

From a perspective of history I can understand the evolution of awareness in this country, increasing permission to let a child be a person. I heard a delightful story recently about a little boy whose parents took him out to eat. When the waitress came to take their orders the child told her, "I want a hot dog, french fries, and a coke." The mother countermanded his order, saying, "Bring him the ground beef, mashed potatoes, and a glass of milk." When the waitress returned she brought the boy a hot dog, french fries, and a coke. The little boy turned to his mother and said, "Gee, Mom, she thinks I'm a real person!"

When parents become aware of more constructive messages and ways of living, they can decide to change their ways of behaving and teach their children new messages. Awareness, I believe, is the key to change. In fact, I regard awareness as the goal of humanity. Awareness is perceiving the here and now without a list of "shoulds" to obscure the reality of the experience. Alan Watts in *The Wisdom of Insecurity*, defines awareness as light: "Light . . . means awareness—to be aware of life, of experience as it is at this moment, without any judgments or ideas about it. In other words, you have to see and feel what you are experiencing as it *is* and not as it is named."* Unfortunately most people let no light shine into the darkness of their lives. Never are they aware enough to see clearly without their mental shoulds to obscure their vision. Nor do they give their children permission to experience and respond to life as it *is*.

Darren S. had been born to an older couple who lived an isolated life. His father, retired early from the Army, did little else other than watch TV. His mother, a depressed and silent woman, preferred to sleep during the day and stay up all night. The family had no friends that Darren could remember and saw no one socially. Darren's mother was so fearful of leaving their house that she rarely went out. His father handled all business outside the home, including the grocery shopping. This was his one social activity and his

---

*Alan Watts, *The Wisdom of Insecurity* (New York, Vintage Books, A Division of Randolph House, Inc., 1941), pp. 75-6.

only chance to communicate with others. Not wanting to be bothered he rarely took Darren along on these shopping trips. Darren had no companions as a small child and little contact with anyone other than his parents.

"The only words my mother ever said to me were, 'Don't do this. Don't do that.' " Darren told me. "She always seemed angry because I was there. And my father never wanted me to interrupt his TV programs. I remember trying to play with him and climb on him until I was about six. Then I gave up."

In his adaptation to his parents' demands, Darren learned isolation. In order to be accepted by them he learned to live within himself and intrude upon them as little as possible. He decided that it was not okay to express himself because his mother criticized him and his father ignored him, so he learned to say nothing. He kept his eyes downcast and distrusted any attempt at intimacy.

When I met Darren he was twenty-six years old, lived alone, had never dated a girl, and had no close friends. He was in one of my groups for over a year before he dared meet my eyes or begin to share his early life experiences. His adaptive mechanism had been appropriate to his parents' demands, ensuring his early survival within the climate of a family isolated from one another. Later on it had robbed him of enjoying people around him and knowing intimacy of any kind. Darren's role as an isolated child had continued into that of a grown-up hermit.

The symbiotic relationship between children and their parents can be a healthy spur to growth if children are given enough love and freedom to be themselves. They will be able to untie symbiotic bonds as they mature and replace them with self-reliance. But if parents do not respect children as persons in their own rights, expecting them instead to conform to parental commands, such children may never develop the sense of Self. They may keep demanding that parents love them and recognize them as persons, holding tighter to the symbiotic bond the older they grow. For the rest of their lives they may relate to others in the same role in which they learned to relate to their parents. Thomas Wolfe wrote a book called *You Can't Go Home Again*, dealing with one person's inability to recapture the childhood and home he remembered. Some children, on the contrary, never leave home and parents, no matter where in the world they live. They carry them around forever, inside their heads.

Laura May W. had been severely abused as a child. She had been born and raised on an isolated mountain farm in Appalachia. Her father was more interested in his whiskey still than the farm; consequently they were very poor. He sold very little of his whiskey to others; he was his own best customer. When he was drunk, which was almost daily, he forced himself sexually upon one or more of his four daughters. Laura May could not remember when it started; she thought she was probably three or four years old. If she or her sisters objected, her father beat them and threatened to kill them. So Laura May learned to submit to him. Her mother, an extremely passive individual, feigned ignorance of what was happening, even though she would conduct the girls into the bedroom when her husband demanded to see them.

Laura May hated her father for abusing her and her mother for not protecting her from him. She tried to tell some relatives and friends about her father on several occasions, but no one listened. Either no one believed her or they just didn't care. Laura May's father threatened to have her put in jail if she ever told the authorities. He said she was evil for doing what she did with him and if the police ever found out it would be too bad. When she was about ten, she ran away, intending to get to town somehow and tell her story to the police. But town was too far to walk, and she eventually turned around and went back home, knowing nowhere else to go. Once a minister who was passing by stopped and asked her why she looked so sad.

"Is there something wrong with your family life?" he asked with concern. "Aren't you happy living at home? Tell me what's wrong, my child."

"You wouldn't believe me if I told you," she said.

"Of course I would," he replied.

So she said, "Okay, I'll tell you. My father has sex with me every day, sometimes two or three times a day."

"I don't believe you," the minister said, walking off.

From that time on the only way she rebelled against her father was by getting sick and going to bed, usually with a bad headache. She had learned that if she was sick, he might leave her alone.

Finally, when she was twenty, she and another sister hitched a ride on a passing wagon and went to the city. They found jobs as waitresses and never returned home. Laura May never saw or heard from her parents again, but she could not leave their memory behind.

Leaving home did not cure her physical problems either. When she came to me she was having a least one migraine a week that kept her incapacitated for two or three days. She had been to many doctors, none of whom could give her permanent relief. She was losing hope of ever being well. She also suffered from continual depression. She told me the story of her past quite readily.

"Are you still angry at your father for abusing you all those years," I asked.

"Oh, no," she said. "I hated him for many years but I've worked all that out by now. I can understand some of his reasons now. I'm not angry at anyone, just myself. I'm so ugly." At this point she began to cry. "I hate myself," she said.

I did not believe that she had let her anger go, because she still had such strong negative messages in her head. She had long ago accepted the role her father had given her of being a bad girl, entirely to blame for his sexual advances. Therefore, when she dealt with people in the here and now, the messages he originally gave her kept running through her brain: "You're ugly," "You're bad," "You're to blame," "You'll never make it on your own." The messages continued until Laura May became so depressed she would go to bed with a headache to get her father off her back, just as she had done when she was living at home.

It did not surprise me that she had married a man who put her down. He did not beat her as her father had done, but he gave her many of the same messages, which she accepted and believed—messages of worthlessness, helplessness, and blame. And she felt the old feelings that she had felt as a child—sick, angry, and hurt. Though she was angry at her husband continuously during their fifteen-year marriage, she feared expressing her feelings to him because she believed her misery was all her fault. She handled her anger towards him in the same way she had handled it towards her father; she buried it inside herself. I explained to her that her depression was made up of retroflected anger, that is, anger she felt towards someone else, did not dare express directly to him, and consequently reflected back onto herself.

"You mean depression is only anger turned inwards?" she asked.

"Yours is, isn't it?" I responded.

"Yes," she said, "I am furious at my husband."

And she discovered that she was still furious at her father. She spent many therapy sessions sobbing in helpless rage, gradually releasing her feelings through the tears she had never allowed herself to pour out.

I learned to ask Laura May about her earlier experiences whenever she would report having a pain in her head. In this way we discovered that she had a time lag for her feelings. When an upsetting event occurred, she did not allow herself to feel or express her anger; it was about one week after such events that her migraine headaches and depression attacks would result. Through her work in therapy, she learned to shorten her time lag to the point where she can now feel and express her anger in direct response to many annoying situations.

During her therapy Laura May was able to get in touch with her anger toward her mother as well as her father, and release her feelings through tears. She also learned to express her feelings verbally. She gave up her migraines as the inner tension caused by her anger lessened. She still gets depressed and feels pressure in her head when she does not express her anger directly but she no longer experiences the extreme pain. She now understands how completely she had adapted to her father's programming. He had convinced her that she was to blame for his sexual advances and that she was evil. He enforced this belief by the physical pain of beatings and the emotional anguish of making her submit to him. Since she was prohibited from expressing her anger to her father, her only defenses were numbing her bodily feelings during the sex act or becoming depressed and sick.

"That was very smart of you," I said. "You survived a childhood some kids would not have been able to."

"It wasn't smart of me at all," she argued. "It was dumb not to see what was really happening."

"You saw what was happening," I said. "And you took an

effective means of fighting it. What would have happened if you had really fought back physically or refused to do what he wanted?"

"He'd have killed me," she said.

"Right. He would have beaten you, perhaps to the point of death. So you adapted to the situation, believed what he wanted you to believe, and survived. Good for you."

"It was dumb," she insisted.

"No," I said. "It was appropriate at the time. Now it is no longer appropriate. What can you do now instead of hating yourself and depressing yourself because of it?"

"I can let myself feel my feelings and, when I'm angry at someone, tell him about it."

And indeed she did. She told her husband about her anger toward him. She eventually divorced him, something she had wanted to do for years. She began to express her anger when it was appropriate—toward women first because they were not quite as threatening to her, then toward men. Instead of continuing to be ruled by her father's demands that she play the role of an ugly, evil, subservient girl, she is on the road to relying on herself for her own existence. She has lost the strained, hostile look with which she used to face the world. Now her face seems fuller because she is less tense; she smiles often and, when she is feeling good, has the appearance of an assured, beautiful woman.

I wish I could say that Laura May has conquered all her problems and is now happy. Unfortunately I cannot. She suffered so much trauma in her childhood from her crazy, violent father that she has farther to go in attaining mental health than the average person. She has come a long way in feeling better about herself, but she is still acting out her basic struggle with her father by choosing male friends who put her down. This behavior only causes her to feel miserable and depress herself.

"Why," she has asked me, "do I keep picking these domineering bastards instead of somebody who will treat me decently?" I could never give her the answer to that excellent question. To find her own solution she must trace back her childhood feelings so that she can split that original symbiotic bond.

Laura May had related to her father as a scared child to a vicious parent. His continual abuse was all she had ever known of parental love. Therefore, when she thought of love, she got a picture in her head of oppressive control, abuse, and negative criticism. When she picked a male companion, she chose him for exactly those qualities. Furthermore, she also had in her head the memory of her mother's behavior. She followed her mother's example of passivity in response to the abuse she got.

One day she complained about Ben, her current lover, a hard drinking, explosive man. "He went out with another woman, and I knew it. So I decided to go out too. When I told him what I had done he gave me hell and said he expected me to sit home and wait for him or he would give it to me. That's not fair!"

"How would you have felt," I asked, "if he had said instead, 'That's really neat that you went out without me. I hope you had a good time!' "

"Why, the louse," she said without a moment's hesitation. "I would have felt he didn't care."

"Right," I said. "Whereas if he gives you hell and orders you to sit home and wait for him, what do you feel?"

"I feel cared about and that makes me okay," she said in amazement. "But that's crazy. I'm so miserable when he treats me like that. I don't want that."

"You may not want to be treated like that, but that is just what you're asking for when you choose a man like Ben. Now, what's involved in changing that kind of choice?"

"I guess I'd have to feel okay to begin with," she said in a small voice. "Then I wouldn't need a man to make me feel okay."

"Let's go back to the beginning," I said. "Your feelings are your own; no one can *make* you feel."

"I am responsible for my own feelings," she said. "Oh, that's so hard to learn. I say it and say it and sometimes I believe it but I guess I still don't believe it all the way."

"What do you feel when you don't have a man around?" I asked.

"I feel scared," she said, "and lonely. I know I won't be able to make it on my own."

"You feel scared and lonely, just as you used to feel when you were a kid, but knowing you won't make it is your belief, not your feeling," I maintained. "Isn't that just what your father used to tell you in order to control you?"

"Yes," she said, "I always wanted him to love me and treat me well but he never did. He insisted I do exactly what he wanted and if I didn't he beat me."

"You still want men to love you and treat you well, don't you?" I asked.

"Of course," she said. "Doesn't everyone?"

"What if you *never* find a man who will love you the way you want to be loved. What will happen to you?"

"I don't know," she said. "That's scary to think about."

"Think about it," I insisted. "What will happen to you if you never find the love you're looking for. Will you survive?"

"Oh, I guess I'd survive all right. But I wouldn't like it. It would be hard."

"How hard?" I asked. "What would you do?"

"I just don't know," she said.

"Would you fall down in a faint and die of a broken heart?"

"Of course not," she said. "Now you're being silly."

"Then what would you do?" I asked.

"I'd feel scared and lonely and I'd cry a lot," she said.

"For how long?" I asked. "A year?"

"No, not that long," she said. "Off and on, just like I do now."

"Could you survive that?" I asked.

"Yes," she said. "I'd survive. I've felt that way all of my life and I've survived. It's tough but I've made it."

"Yes, you have, haven't you?" I said. "Good for you. So, if you know that you have survived all these years and that you can survive many more, even without a man, what do you think you still need a man around for?"

She thought about that for a minute, then she said. "You're right. I don't need a man to make it. I guess I can make it on my own because I already have. Yes, I think I can."

"I don't believe you," I said.

"I don't believe myself," she answered.

"What do you feel inside your body when you feel scared and lonely?" I asked.

She got in touch with her pain and allowed it to flow out through her tears. Finally she took a deep breath.

"I know I can make it now," she said. "Even though at times I know I will still doubt myself and feel bad, right now I really believe

I can make it. And I'm going to keep right on believing it, so take that, Dad!"

"Hooray for you!" I exclaimed. "I believe you too. It's not every day you split your symbiotic bond."

Laura May is still working on her redecision, some days feeling solid and sure of her ability to survive on her own, other days feeling shaky and scared about it. That symbiotic bond is not split forever in a day. It takes years to be formed; sometimes it takes years to lose. It is lost through a process of feeling those painful feelings, deciding, and then redeciding. Once Laura May had made the decision that she would make it, we both knew her fight was not over. Each insight she has gained has helped her to become more aware of where her feelings and decisions originated. The more aware she becomes, the more able she is to redecide how to act her real self. Each time she redecides it becomes a little easier. And each time she allows herself to feel her original fear and pain she lets a little more of those painful childhood feelings go.

She has stopped seeing Ben and has dated several men since. None of them has proven to be the "one and only," but she is not feeling so dependent on men now. The less dependent she feels, the fewer demands she puts on her friends to support her and be what she wants them to be. I am sure that if she keeps on allowing herself to feel her own feelings, someday she will meet a man with whom she can share a healthy, satisfying relationship instead of the destructive kind she has known.

That is great to think about, isn't it—a satisfying relationship, fulfullment, and happiness. And it is possible for you. You can change your role, just as Laura May is changing hers. Think about what you would gain if you did change to become what you really want to be. Happiness? Self-confidence? Intimacy? Freedom? You stand to gain all of these and more. Then why don't you change? You know it is in your power. All of the new schools of therapy claim that it is possible. Our culture has always preached the ability to change. There are countless tales about the poor boy rising to the top, Cinderella finding her prince, the orphan finding a real home at last, the immigrant achieving a "good life." In fact, our culture seems to say, "Anyone can make it who *really* wants to!"

So what is preventing you from achieving what you want?

What stops you from changing? The answer lies not in what you stand to gain, but in what you might lose if you changed. Misery, tension, anger, depression, and loneliness—what do these negative feelings do *for* you? Consider, for example, how such feelings worked for Carol B.

Carol had learned early in her life that it was okay to be angry. As the middle child in a family of three children, she had found that being angry got her a lot of attention, all bad. It was not okay for her to express her feelings verbally but it was accepted by the family that she acted angrily most of the time.

"Carol is pouting again," her mother would explain.

"Cat got your tongue?" her sister would tease.

"Carol is throwing things," her brother would complain.

"Behave yourself, Carol," her mother would scold. "Why can't you act right?"

So Carol learned that even though her unverbalized anger was painful, it provided her with recognition and a kind of uniqueness. This was important to her survival in a large and cramped family. During the Depression her father could not find a job. Carol's family moved in with her mother's parents, along with an uncle and his family. Six adults and seven children lived in one small house for several years, until Carol's father and uncle found work and could afford to move their families out. Carol still remembers the feeling of suffocation she felt in that house; she still feels uncomfortable whenever she is inside a building.

Carol told me one of her memories of feeling suffocated, of the time her family locked her in a closet to deaden the sound of her screams. As her anger became terror no one paid any attention. She could hear her family talking calmly outside while she screamed and sobbed. She also remembers having to stand in the corner for what seemed like hours and being sent to bed without any supper. Through experiences such as these, Carol eventually decided that it did no good to show her family what she was really feeling. They would not recognize her expressions of fear, hurt, or despair. They only seemed to hear her when she screamed in rage. Carol decided that she would never cry in front of them or let them see her fear, only her anger. When she expressed anger her family members responded, both verbally and nonverbally, "That's Carol for you."

So she began to think of herself as an angry child and continued to act accordingly.

Besides being angry, Carol was confused about what was expected of her. With so many adults in the home she received many conflicting messages.

"I got so many 'don'ts' I sometimes have no idea of what I can do," Carol told me. "Don't flush the toilet in the middle of the night and wake people up—don't go to the toilet without flushing it afterwards; Don't leave the window open to let in the cold—don't close the window at night or you'll suffocate; Don't be too friendly—don't be impolite."

She got many nonverbal messages too. Carol remembers these in the sense of, "Don't do what I do, do what I tell you to do."

"Mother would scold me for not cleaning the house in the right way, but she would never clean it well. Her attitude was, 'What's the use with all these kids around?' She would tell me I could do anything I wanted to do in life but she would never show me by her example or help me learn anything. When I asked her what I should do she'd tell me to figure it out myself. Then when I'd try to do something she'd tell me not to do that. I'm scared to try anything now."

When she was nineteen Carol married Walter, a soft-spoken man who disliked any expression of anger. She would rant angrily at him when they had a conflict, and he would get depressed. He would stay in his depression for days sometimes, during which neither would talk to the other. Then they would explode. Their brief but stormy verbal exchange would give them a few moments of intimacy and they would reconcile temporarily. As time went by their periods of silence and depression became longer and longer. When they came to me they were on the verge of separation.

"I'm angry all the time," Carol said during one session. "At everyone—my husband, my kids, myself, the whole world. I won't do anything, even housework. I don't have any skills to get a job. I don't know what to do."

"You're feeling stuck," I suggested.

"Yes, I am," she agreed, "and I'm screaming mad about it inside."

"What would you gain if you weren't angry all the time?" I asked.

"We'd have a happy family. We'd be able to talk together rationally instead of screaming at each other or not talking at all. I could do something with my life. We wouldn't be so depressed."

"How would you feel if you had this kind of life?"

"Oh, free, I guess," she said vaguely. "Content inside, happy."

"What would you lose if you weren't angry?"

"My anger, of course," she snapped. "My bitchiness, my intolerance, my fits of rage; nothing I want to hang onto."

"I question that," I said. "Let's do an exercise to get you in touch with your feelings. Imagine that you're a child again, about five or six. Tell me about some time you got angry then."

She closed her eyes and went back in her memory. "I remember once my sister had a birthday; I must have been five and she was three. She got a new dress. I don't know where they got the money for it in those days. They put it on her and everybody stood around saying how pretty she was in it. I was furious. I was jealous of her anyway because I always thought she was prettier than me. I got so angry I poured my lemonade all over that dress. They made me go in the closet and they locked the door so they wouldn't hear me scream."

"What are you feeling?" I asked.

"Boiling mad," she said. "I hate them, I can't stand them all telling me how bad I am. I want to tear them all apart."

I shut up while she got into her feelings. After she opened her eyes I said, "Now imagine the same scene but, instead of getting angry and doing what you did, you're happy and join in. What do you feel?"

"Terrible," she replied. "I'm not happy; I'm only pretending to be happy. I really feel dead, as if they had just swallowed me up and I'm being digested. In fact, I'm not even there; they aren't seeing me." She opened her eyes in amazement. "My anger helps me feel alive, proves that I exist. If I didn't have that I wouldn't be anybody!"

"That sounds like a pretty valuable feeling," I said. "Your anger gets you attention and even if that's a negative kind of attention it's better than none at all. Are you sure you want to give that up?"

She thought about it for a moment. "I don't want to give up my feelings of being alive but I still want to get rid of my anger. There must be a better way of proving my existence."

"There is," I agreed. "What do you think it is?"

"Express my feelings as I feel them?" she said hesitantly.

"Right on," I said.

"That's scary," she said. "It never did me any good to express my feelings when I was a kid. Nobody listened and that hurt worse than keeping them inside. Besides, if I really came out and said exactly what I felt now, Walter would leave me."

"He might," I said. "Of course, if you go on the way you're going now he will leave you anyway. You're already considering separation, if not divorce. So which is worse—feeling scared and taking the risk that Walter will leave by telling him what you feel, or not expressing your feelings and making sure that he leaves you?"

"Not expressing myself is worse," she said. And slowly, painfully, she began to act on that decision by revealing her fear and anguish, even allowing herself to cry in front of others. Walter supported her in her decision and worked alongside her to increase his awareness of his own feelings. He began to express his own anger rather than depress himself by holding it in. They began to achieve longer and longer periods of intimacy and communication. Carol continued to work on her own growth by taking classes in dance therapy. She found herself getting in touch with feelings of pure joy for the first time in her life. In moving without limitations she experienced a sense of freedom she had never felt before. She discovered that she could actually feel happy.

Both Laura May and Carol had responded to their families' demands, the former by adapting to those demands, the latter by rebelling against them. Carol found that she had adapted, in a sense, even in her rebellion. She did not feel free to pursue her own life but felt compelled to continually rebel against all commands, constructive and destructive alike. "Why should I?" was her usual response to any message she heard as a command. The "shoulds" in her head were so strong she heard them in the most innocuous of messages and reacted with anger. It was Carol, in her angry days, who had responded to my "Have a good week," with, "I will if I want to!" If she wanted to do something and someone told her to do just that, she would not, even though she was the one who suffered by not doing it.

As Carol began to express her feelings her physical appearance changed. Her eyes seemed less wild and her face looked softer. Her movements became more fluid, and she laughed her short, bitter laugh less often. As with Laura May, feedback from others speeded her change. When Laura May and Carol held in their anger they still looked and acted in a hostile manner, inviting others to respond angrily. "What's the matter with me?" Carol had asked me once. "Why do people pick on me?"

When she began to change, she gave out fewer hostile messages; consequently people "picked on" her less. She began to realize that people had only been giving back what she had been sending out. The better she felt about herself, the more she was able to act in a relaxed and nonjudgmental manner, and the more people responded with warmth and openness.

Laura May and Carol and Darren and Marv all chose to adapt to their families' demands in order to survive. Darren adapted by becoming silent and withdrawn. Marv adapted by becoming mama's good, nonsexual boy. Laura May adapted by depressing herself and having migraine attacks. Carol adapted by acting hostile and rebelling against every command, no matter how inconsequential. They were all taught to play their roles by verbal instructions and non-verbal direction. Darren was taught by indifference from his father and reprimands from his mother. Laura May was taught by beatings and sexual abuse from her father and her mother's passivity. Carol was taught by her father's inattention and her mother's helpless rage. Marv was taught by his mother's disapproval and his father's submission. They played their respective roles within their families and continued to play them out of habit after leaving home. They knew no other roles. These people were miserable playing their roles but they knew what their parents expected and they continued to act accordingly. Just because they had left their family homes years ago did not mean they had been able to leave behind their parents' messages and examples. Their old patterns of response were familiar to them, as was the old fear of being abandoned.

No other fear can approach the fear of abandonment for a child, not even the fear of dying. No child understands death but all children appreciate and fear the consequences of being left by their parents. If a person has often experienced being abandoned as a child those childhood feelings may prevail throughout adult life. Such a person may continue to act out destructive roles for a lifetime because the fear of abandonment is so strong.

Some children have not actually been abandoned by their parents but have been threatened with abandonment. The effect may be the same. One client told me her mother used to threaten to leave forever when the children misbehaved. To back up her threat, the mother would drive off in the car for a short time that seemed to the wailing children an eternity. Other people have remembered their parents threatening "If you don't behave I'll send you to an orphanage," or "I'll give you away," or "The bogeyman will get you if you're not good." One woman told me that her mother used to tie her outside on the porch, even in winter, with the threat that she would be left there for good if she did not behave.

So when I hear people say they are afraid to express their real feelings "because she might leave me," or even "because they might not like me," I know their fears are related to the archetypal fear of being abandoned. I have heard this corroborated by class after class in my experience as a teacher. In one group exercise exploring self-assertion in a variety of situations, the one consistently fearful situation is that in which one is rejected. Again I hear this as the fear of being abandoned.

One feeling that I often hear clients express is that of jealousy. When I hear the word, "jealous," I listen for feelings of abandonment. One woman told me of her particular terror of abandonment. When her husband was away, even on an overnight business trip, she felt an overwhelming panic and invariably called him several times "to make sure he was still there." He accused her of distrusting him. She could never explain to him that it was not really distrust of him that choked her with fear. When we traced her feeling back to her childhood she discovered several occasions when she had felt abandoned, the worst being the death of her father when she was five years old. Other people describing jealous feelings to me have also been able to trace them back into their childhood and dicover instances of feeling abandoned. They may not have been abandoned in actuality but they experienced enough parental neglect and inattention that they *felt* abandoned.

I do not mean to say that all feelings of jealousy are based on fears of abandonment. There is another kind of jealousy, one based on feelings of competition. One woman expressed to me such jealousy when she said, "I was jealous of my brother because he could go places I couldn't." I prefer to call such feelings "envy" instead of "jealousy." Envy to me has more anger in it, while the jealousy of abandonment has more fear.

Carol B. gave her archaic childhood fear a grownup meaning when she said she was afraid to express her real feelings to Walter because he might abandon her. No matter that they were already considering divorce; she still feared that he would leave her if she was open with him. Irrational? Of course. There is little rationale to feelings. One just feels. And sometimes only in tracing the feeling back into the shadows of the past does any logical reason appear. Laura May expressed a similar dread of abandonment when she told me of her fear that she could not make it on her own without a man. It didn't matter to her that she already was surviving on her own. She was still feeling the old fear that she might be left alone.

These people worked on experiencing their childhood feelings in order to understand their early decisions. They made new decisions to discard their old familiar but destructive roles. By gaining insight into the history of their roles they have changed their old patterns of response into behavior more appropriate for the here and now.

Change can be achieved in another way, however. By first changing your role and then staying in touch with your feelings as you act it out, you may discover new feelings. If the role feels comfortable and you like the responses it brings you from others, you may decide to keep it. If it feels wrong for you, drop it and try another. Remember that your new role may feel uncomfortable at first even if your behavior in it is open, free, and entirely appropriate. You are used to your old role; you have been wearing it like a worn-out shoe, cracks and all. You cannot take it off in a day. Change takes time. If you are trying on a new role for size, decide to give it a fair try. As you encounter your archaic, painful childhood feelings, go ahead and experience them, *and* stay with your role. If you decide that the role is not You after a few weeks of exploring it in depth, you can create another, for the roles we play are limited only by our imagination.

You may believe that you are free to be who you want to be in your present role, and you may be right. But if in your present role you are rebelling against the demands of others, you are not free to be your own feeling, unfettered self. Certainly you are not free if you are adapting to the demands of others and striving desperately to please them. Perhaps you can achieve that sense of freedom by creating an entirely new role for yourself. Or you may surprise yourself by realizing that your old role, compared to the new one, is not so bad after all. You may discover that you can be who you want to be when you accept the person you already are.

4

Role therapy

*We can write
new roles for ourselves.*

Drama began in ancient Greece as the ritual enactment of the time-less stories of gods and mortal heroes that had been handed down from generation to generation since the dawn of history. Two types of drama were developed by the ancient Greeks, tragedy and com-edy. Although no one today knows exactly when either comedy or tragedy began, historical experts tend to agree that drama evolved over a long period of time, as the ancients became more and more aware of the difference between the symbolic acts of their rituals and "real life," and between the actors and the roles they were playing.

Actors in ancient Greek drama wore costumes with elaborate masks. These masks helped the actors to be seen and recognized by members of the audience, some of whom sat quite a distance away. The masks enabled the actors to immediately establish their iden-tities. They represented well-known character types, not meant to portray ordinary people. The tragic masks were intended to create the illusion of extraordinary heroes and gods. The comic masks created exaggerated caricatures of the roles they represented. Both types of masks removed the actors from ordinary humanity. They served as disguises, behind which the real faces of the actors were completely hidden.

Like the ancient Greeks, we who act in the theatre of life use masks to make ourselves instantly recognizable to others. If we have been taught that it is not okay to be who we are and express what we feel, we mold our masks to illustrate the roles we have decided to play. We play countless roles—the nice guy, the bitch, the martyr, the hypochondriac, the hard worker, the nervous type, the strong man, the joker, the boss, the helpless lady, the dummy, and so on. These roles affect the way we act and the way we look; the mask takes its toll on the whole body. The nice guy smiles, the hard worker frowns, the martyr stoops, the nervous type twitters, and the dummy shrugs. The body itself becomes fixed after years of conforming to a mold. The smile becomes etched as does the frown, the stoop becomes a humped back, the shrug evolves into permanently uplifted shoulders. We become our masks.

As the ancient Greeks used masks to separate the characters in the drama from ordinary people, we use masks to detach ourselves from our own humanity. We not only hide from others behind our masks, we hide from ourselves. We become the role we play and lose awareness of our essential being. We begin to ask the question, "Who am I?" Alexander Lowen explains this identity crisis as a split between the ego and the body:

> The child who is forced to conform to a parent's unconscious image loses his sense of self, his feeling of identity, and his contact with reality. . . . In attempting to fulfill his own image, he feels frustrated and cheated of emotional satisfaction. The image is an abstraction, an ideal, and an idol which demands the sacrifice of personal feeling. The image is a mental conception which, superimposed on the physical being, reduces bodily existence to a subsidiary role. The body becomes an instrument of the will in the service of the image. The individual is alienated from the reality of his body.*

What can we do about our identity crises? How can we take off our masks and reclaim our essential beings? How can we find our feeling selves? I have discussed earlier some of the reasons we assume roles. We learn, over a period of years, how to play these

*Alexander Lowen, M.D., *The Betrayal of the Body* (New York, Collier Books, a Division of Macmillan Pub. Co., Inc. 1967), pp. 4-5.

roles and which masks to wear. Is it not reasonable then to think that we can learn new roles, roles which feel right as we act them out? Is it not reasonable to think that we can relearn, through new roles, how to express our feeling selves? Perhaps we can go back to the drama in order to do this, drama in this case enacted in the theatre of life.

Actors on stage know that they can get into the feelings of a character by acting out that role. My understanding of "getting into a role" began with the often repeated principle of one of my professors in graduate school: "Drama is character in action." I began to realize that when I act a role I become that character—moving, appearing, thinking, and feeling as that character might. I put myself into the role and become the character as I imagine her to be. My feelings, too, change as I become a different person.

I remember acting out the part of a middle-aged, poverty-stricken, disheartened black woman in one play. As I got into the role I was surprised at my feelings of apathy and fatigue. I even found myself walking and moving ponderously, as if I were weighted down by some enormous, tangible burden. That character was one I was glad to leave behind me when the play was over. It took me several weeks to drop some of the negative feelings I experienced in the role. I was happy to see them go. If the role had been fun for me, however, I might have chosen to retain some of its characteristics.

Some therapists have seen the value of using role-playing as a tool to help clients gain a feeling for other behavior traits. George Kelly was among the first to use this type of therapy with clients who wished to change their image. He observed:

> The experience of taking a particular part in a dramatic production had frequently had a lasting effect upon the behavior and manner of adjustment of a particular student. For example, there was the high-school friend in a midwestern community who when he went to college, was given the opportunity of playing the part of the English Lord in the play *Dulcy*. . . . Twenty years later he still had the incongruous accent and, as it seemed to the writer, many mannerisms dating precisely from the play.*

*George Kelly, "Fixed Role Therapy," *The Psychology of Personal Constructs*, Chapter 8, V. 1 (New York, Norton Publishing Co., 1955), p. 126.

Kelly did not dismiss the behavior changes he observed in his friend as being simply "affectation." After thinking about it he decided that the change was, "actually a faithful expression of his general outlook."

Howard Blatner, another therapist who has done extensive work in "psychodrama," states: "Taking active and creatively spontaneous role behaviors in many dimensions fulfills an extremely important function: that of validating the sense of one's own vitality, will, authenticity, feelings, imagery, and, in short, the sense of being deeply alive, of being a 'self'."*

George Kelly used the term "fixed-role therapy" to describe his work with clients on new role images. He and his staff wrote "fixed-role sketches" which "invited the client to explore certain sharply contrasting behaviors."† I prefer the simpler term "role therapy." I create new roles not exactly opposite but certainly contrasting with the old ones, flexible rather than fixed. I make a role as flexible as possible, to allow for maximum individual interpretation. If it does not fit at all or if the role player does not like it, the role can always be changed. Few things in life are truly "fixed."

In my experience with role therapy I have found that two things may happen when you begin to act out a role different from your own. You may find that your new role is very similar to your present role, but that it allows even more freedom of expression. Or, you may find that the new role helps you gain an understanding of a new and different way of behavior which you may decide to adopt. Your old role has been built over the years by decisions about how to act, feedback from others, and familiar feelings within that role. If you can be shown new behavior traits, you may use those traits as building blocks with which to create a more positive self image.

Your old role has also been established by a lifetime of behaving in particular ways. Not only have you accepted your role; other people around you have accepted it and anticipate that you will continue to act in the same way. When you start to change they will probably resist your efforts. They will tend to treat you according to

*Howard Blatner, *Acting In: Practical Applications of Psychodramatic Methods* (New York, Springer Publications, 1973), p. 126.

†Kelly, p. 371.

your old role, which in turn makes it more difficult for you to change. In his work with adolescents, David Viscott observed:

> People often change in adolescence or just after adolescence because they do get out of the house and away from people who think of them in one way and expect them to react that way. When young people move to another place, or go to school and find new friends and meet new people who don't have the same old prejudices about them as the people in their past, they are freer to try out new roles without being expected to act a certain way. They are free to grow.*

The value of acting out a role contrasting with your present one is that you are fully aware it is only a practice session. There are no "should" and "ought to be" involved. You are not told that this character is what you should become or that you ought to be this way forever. It is simply a way to practice acting differently than you have acted in the past. You have the security of "make-believe" to fall back on. You can use this technique as the ancient Greeks used the mask—to gain an image and help you get into the feel of the character, but also to hide You. You are not really the person you are pretending to be. You know you are only playacting; if you do not like the role, you can drop it at any time. Or, you can choose to use it or parts of it from now on if you like, and make it your own.

I can already hear some of your objections to my proposal: "She's telling me to act a phony role"; "I'm looking for the real me, not another role act"; "I want to be intimate, not learn more manipulations." I hear you and I can understand your objections. Yet I believe that my proposal is still valid, despite these objections. Your present role may be the phony one. And it may not. The way to find out is to act out a new role while staying aware of your feelings. Your feelings count. Only by checking out what you are feeling inside while you are acting the new role will you be able to discover the validity of the role for you. And is it not worth a try to find out which is more real—your present role or one you have yet to explore?

What is your present role? How could you describe the different roles, or variations of a role, that you play? To find out, quickly list at least ten words that describe you. I might start my list, for

---

*David S. Viscott, *The Making of a Psychiatrist* (New York, Arbor House Publishing Co., Inc., 1972), pp. 146-7.

example, with nouns: woman, wife, mother, teacher, therapist. Then I might go on with adjectives: serious, productive, witty, curious, determined. My list would change from day to day as my feelings change. If I felt depressed and not okay my list would be different. A few years ago my list would have contained words such as: anxious, blue, failure, divorcee, and unhappy. I would have been all too ready to change those role traits into others if I had known how. And it is possible to change roles or certain parts of roles. A great deal of what you are is based on what you believe about yourself. Change your belief system, change the names you call yourself, and you can change your role.

It is important that you pick a role that contrasts sharply with your own. If you pick one that is too similar to the one you already play, you may not be able to feel any difference. So even though a contrasting role may not be what you would like to become in all aspects, try it on for size. There are an infinite number of different roles you can choose. If you do not like one, try another. After all, it is only make-believe.

To create a role for yourself, first write out a short character sketch of yourself as you are now. Be as honest as you can; you need not show it to anyone else. Then pick out about six negative words or phrases that are contained in your character sketch. Quickly now, without thinking about it too hard, write down six words that contrast with the six you have chosen. They may be opposite to the ones you have picked but they do not have to be exact opposites. They may be contrasting in an imaginative way. A dictionary or thesaurus is of great value for this process. Now fill in a characterization around these six contrasting words. As an example, you might write of yourself:

> I am a middle-aged housewife with no purpose in life other than to keep house for my husband and three teenagers. I am <u>fat</u> and <u>dowdy</u> and wear <u>sloppy house-dresses</u> most of the time. I am <u>depressed a lot</u>, <u>smile</u> most of the time even when I'm very angry, and <u>find little fun</u> in life. I don't like myself much and don't know what tomorrow can hold for me.

I have underlined six words you might pick to work with from this brief sketch, which are listed with some contrasting words that might be substituted:

fat	thin, personable, attractive
dowdy	neat, sophisticated, interesting
sloppy house-dresses	floating chiffons, clothes with special flair, accessories
depressed	cheerful, expressive, self-actualizing
smile	serious, real, assertive
little fun	much fun, childlike, impetuous sense of fun

Do not spend time worrying about whether or not your choice of contrasting words is "right." Remember that this sketch is not the person you "should" be. It is only a person you *could* be, one whose traits you are exploring. You will find out if the role "hangs together" and whether or not you like it when you start to act it out.

Now write the new characterization to fit the key words or phrases you have decided on. A sample sketch using contrasting, rather than opposite words, might be:

> I am an attractive woman whom others find extremely interesting to talk to. (Why do they?) I enjoy delving into a variety of subjects and conversing about them. I also listen as intently as I can to what others tell me. I love to dress originally. I use accessories as a special touch to perk up the plainest of outfits. I am a self-actualizing person. (What does that mean?) Even though my major activity is keeping house for my family, I am continually taking classes and reading to improve myself. I do these things, not to please anyone else, but because I want to do them and I believe I am important. I am assertive with my family as well as my friends; people know where they are with me because I tell them what I'm feeling. I have an impetuous sense of fun. (How is it shown?) I may decide on impulse to take a barefoot run on the beach with my teenagers or go with a friend to a movie on the spur of the moment or pack a picnic basket and ask my husband for lunch in the park. Life is fun for me because I am fun.

Now pick a name for your sketch. Again, do not spend too much time picking the "right" name. Just pick one that suggests the character you have written down. If you decide later that it does not seem to fit, you are free to change it. Using the name in your head is

like the dramatic technique of using a mask. It suggests the character and also gives you a cover of pretense to hide behind. You know
that "Jane Summers," or whichever name you pick, is not really
you. If she does something you would not do, you know you are only
pretending to be her. You do not have to lay yourself on the line and
berate yourself if your new role does not turn out the way you would
have liked.

Check out your role by taking a fantasy trip. I have used an
exercise in my classes which can give you a feeling for your role
before you actually start to act it out. Pick one negative word from
your character sketch and substitute a contrasting or opposite word
to counter it, for example, "interesting" for "dowdy." Now go on a
fantasy trip in your head, imagining how you would feel as this new
and "interesting" person in a variety of situations. How would you
walk, talk, laugh, or cry? How would you feel about others and
relate to them? What might you wear? What might be your career?
What would you do for play? Whom might you engage in these
activities with? How would your body feel as this new person—your
stomach, your head, your shoulders, your arms, your legs, all of
you? What would your facial expression convey? What would your
posture be like? Now, as this new character, go into the future ten
years from today. What might you feel like in ten years? What
would you be doing? What would you have accomplished? As you do
this fantasy exercise you will gain a feel for your character that may
encourage you to act out the role or suggest that you choose another
that might be more fun to try.

If you want to act out the character after trying the role out in
fantasy, practice being that person. You do not have to tell anyone
what you are doing. Sometimes it is more revealing to just pretend
to be your new role for a couple of weeks, then ask your family and
friends if they have noticed any changes in you. Read your role over
several times a day and think about how your new character might
act in the situations you encounter in your daily life. How would
your character speak and walk? What would she eat and drink?
What would she do for activities? What would she say to people?
You can see a whole new world through her eyes. Try it on for size.
You might find that you fit into it more happily than into your
present world!

I became acquainted with this facet of drama therapy at Bakker's Adult Development Program in Seattle. As a prospective playwright and drama student I was asked to help the staff write character sketches. Participants would then act out the roles for several weeks, getting daily feedback from other Program members. As some of the participants began acting their roles I was amazed at their changes. I remember one woman who was quiet, sad, unassuming, and always dressed in drab clothes. When she played out her role she dressed flamboyantly, changed her hairdo, spoke before she was spoken to, told jokes, and became the life of the party. I hardly recognized her; she had a totally different presence. Other people made equally drastic changes in their behavior. Since that time I have valued the use of role therapy in helping clients change their self-image. I do not use this kind of therapy with all clients. Some people would find no benefit in working on role changes; they need more extensive work on their feelings. But for certain individuals, role therapy provides an immediate method for gaining a new self-concept.

To give you an idea of the various roles I have used with my clients, I will provide some examples. I asked each person to write out a short characterization sketch. Some wrote several pages; others wrote only a few words. I have included excerpts from some of their sketches to give you a further idea of the kind of sketch you might write.

Irene W. was a forty-five-year-old housewife when she entered my class. She was bored with her life. One teenage boy was already in college; the other would be going soon. Her husband had an engrossing job and many work-related friends. Facing an empty nest, she felt lonely and no longer needed. She wrote:

> People tell me I am not aggressive enough. Perhaps my inferiority feelings block my mind and I can't think of the right answer at the right time. I would really like to be a poised and aggressive person, charming and at ease in all situations. Also, I'd like to be able to express my feelings instead of stifling them and then staying mad for months. I'd like to do something with my appearance. It's dull, my self-image is negative and my personality boring. And I am bored with life.

For the six terms I selected from Irene's sketch, I made the following substitutions:

inferiority	spontaneity
can't think	disagree
staying mad	quick temper
dull	a pleasure
negative	sense of humor
boring	impulsive

From these substitutions, I wrote a new role for Irene, which I called "Merilee."

I am Merilee. I am a pleasure to be with because I find joy in living. I prefer the lighter side of life and can usually find some humor in the dullest of events. I do not put others down with my gaiety but usually infect them with my sense of fun. I love life's differences. I expect others to have opinions of their own. I don't become defensive when others differ with me, but usually can agree to disagree. I enjoy cultivating new friends who are unique in themselves rather than just like me.

I love dressing to express Me; I suit the latest fashions to my taste rather than going along with the crowd. I love impulsive shopping trips, exploring my city, having lunch out, candlelight dinners at home, small parties, art, music and conversation. I love people. I have a quick temper and yell a lot when I'm angry. But I get over my "mads" quickly and am ready for fun again. I allow others to get angry and yell at me too. I have many friends who enjoy me as much as I enjoy them. My sense of humor and my spontaneity are my keys to opening the door of the good life. And I do.

Irene started to change as she played out her new role. She began by changing little things in her life: going out of her home more often instead of watching soap operas, trying new grocery stores, going to different churches, exploring new roads in her neighborhood. Eventually she applied for a volunteer job as a museum guide and found that her new image gave her the confidence to get it. Her volunteer work gave her the topics she needed for conversation and introduced her to many new friends. Now she no longer worries about being bored. She has so much to do she barely has time to fit it all in.

Gladys M. was in her early fifties when she came into my therapy group. She had been divorced for several years. Her children were all married and on their own, she had no job skills or hobbies that she enjoyed. She was on welfare and had little hope for her future. For her characterization sketch Gladys wrote:

> I am an unattractive woman, tall and fat, with a mad facial expression. I am very nervous, worry a lot, am emotional, outspoken, very critical of myself and others. I'm scared and depressed over my future. Have more or less given up. I'm tired and disgusted. I guess I expect too much. I don't have confidence in myself, very unorganized. I'm a failure at anything and everything I do or try to do. I hold grudges and have a chip on my shoulder. Have lot of bitterness, heartache, poverty, health problems.

For Gladys, I made the following substitutions:

mad facial expression	warmth
worry a lot	put my total attention on
outspoken	listen
very critical	few expectations
failure	make mistakes
hold grudges	expressing how I feel

I then wrote for her the role of "Bonnie."

> My name is Bonnie. I consider myself a happy woman. My secret ingredient for happiness is that I put my total attention on whatever I am doing at the time. Whether I'm washing dishes or doing macrame, listening to a record or talking to a friend, I give all of myself to my subject. When I talk to someone, I look into his eyes and really listen to what he is saying. I do share my own problems but I don't dwell on them and I don't let them get me down. If I can't solve my problems immediately, I put them aside and involve myself in the Now. I have faith that my waiting is in itself a solution and that I will find the answer by not seeking it. I do make plans for the future but don't worry about whether or not I will do the right thing. I know I am an okay person even when I make mistakes. I do what I can and if it turns out badly, there is always a tomorrow.

> I enjoy people for what they are rather than what they ought to be. I have as few expectations of others as I do of myself. I give them the same privilege I do myself, that of expressing how I feel when I'm feeling it. Others respond to me with feelings, which are sometimes painful to accept. But I strongly believe that it's better to get feelings out as we go than hold them in to ulcerate inside. So even though my feelings and those of others sometimes hurt, I allow their expression. I don't allow hitting, but yelling's okay. I use a lot of facial expression and gestures when I talk to people. And I get warmth in return.

Gladys became aware, as she began to play the role of Bonnie, just how much time she had previously spent in fantasizing. With no children or husband to care for and nothing to do that she considered important she sat day after lonely day in her small apartment, living in her thoughts—not constructive thoughts that would get her on with her life, but the dwelling on past hurts, future anxieties, and present woes that continually dragged her down into depression. One of the first things Gladys did in her new role was to get a job. Because she was a good seamstress herself, and because as Bonnie she could pay attention to what she was interested in, she chose a fabric store as her place of employment. Certainly her job did not solve all of her problems. But it alleviated many of them— loneliness, feelings of worthlessness, and much of her depression. The last I heard from Gladys she was still working and gaining a worthwhile image of herself. She was a far cry from the Gladys I met who had "more or less given up."

Paul G. joined one of my groups as a result of a court order. He was on probation for a charge of indecent exposure. He was then about twenty-five years old, tall, ruggedly handsome, and unusually surly. His marriage was in the process of breaking up. He was confused about his future. He used to sit through the entire group period without saying a word. He seemed resentful for having to come to group as a part of his sentence. Although he refused to talk during group sessions, he willingly wrote out a character sketch.

> I'm quiet yet competitive. I find myself quite often comparing myself with others and usually putting myself at the bottom of the group. This inferiority feeling about myself is probably due to my lack of communicating my emotions with other people. I keep most of my emotions to myself, therefore not letting others know the real me

which makes it hard for me to relate to them and vice versa. I find
that my sense of humor is usually directed at belittling others, although I usually try to keep it to a minimum because I myself dislike
criticism directed at me. I criticize myself enough as it is. I don't feel
at ease talking to people, either to one person or a group.

For Paul I created the role of "Alex," based on the following substitutions:

competitive	fascinated by people
inferiority	at ease with myself
lack of communicating	curiosity
belittling others	easy acceptance of
criticize	think people are great
don't feel at ease	don't feel threatened

The new sketch was quite different than the other.

I am Alex. I am fascinated by people but I can't stay objective about
them. I either really like them and want to be with them or dislike
them and want to avoid them. I have an easy acceptance of those
people I like that allows them to drop their guard and express their
real feelings. In a group or with strangers I am usually the first to
speak up. I sometimes feel shy about speaking but I know that there
are others who are even shyer. So I make the effort and it invariably
pays off in my feeling that I have reached out and touched another
human being. I don't just chitchat, although I can do that if I want to.
Usually I try to contact the person beneath the veneer. And when I
look into a person's eyes I often get the feeling that I have had a peek
into his soul.

Perhaps the key to my personality is my insatiable curiosity about
others. I believe that every person, no matter how dull looking, has
an exciting story to tell. Since I feel at ease with myself, others often
tell me their secrets and their problems. I don't feel threatened when
they open up to me; I look at each person as an interesting individual,
more because of his faults than in spite of them. I find that the more I
listen to people and commiserate with them, the more I can open up
to them about where I'm at. And the more I think people are great
the more I think, "Hey, Alex, old man—you're pretty great yourself!"

Part of the value of enacting a new role in a group setting is that you can practice your role during group and get feedback from other group members. They can make suggestions on different ways you might act out your role or things that your character might do, and give you their insights on whether your acting of the character is appropriate to the role. Paul got into his role one night, much to the surprise of the group. He practiced being Alex and, for the first time, he talked. He talked about his childhood—his father who left home when he was five, his mother who worked all day and was too tired to care for them at night, his two brothers with whom he had little in common. He talked about his problems with his wife and his confusion about the divorce. He talked about his dreams and his frustrations. For once in his life, he communicated. The group responded, praising him for speaking out so openly. They gave him many constructive suggestions on how he might continue to play the role of Alex in his daily life.

Paul did not stay long in group after that. He stopped coming because of a conflict in scheduling with a new job he had taken. When he told me that he could not continue, he sounded sad. He said he was just starting to get something out of group, but he had to earn a living. I have not seen or heard from Paul since. But at least once he made the effort to reach out and touch other people, and to share himself with them. Let's hope that with the help of Alex he still is.

Amy V. took one of my classes because her husband had suggested it might help her gain a more positive self-image. Although she was a lovely young girl and always dressed attractively, she put herself down out of habit. If she did receive a compliment she would blush and find some way to reject it. She was very nervous and spoke in such a tiny voice she could scarcely be heard. She had been married for two years and had no children. She wanted to get a job but was so afraid of being interviewed she would not even apply for one. For her character sketch she wrote:

> I feel very self-conscious speaking or doing things in front of people, even something I know deep down that I can do. I have what you might call an inferiority complex and don't really think I'm worthwhile. I can't make decisions and wonder sometimes how anybody ever gets an opinion; I don't seem to have any. I'm shy talking to people and blush easily. I get so nervous about speaking sometimes I

shake all over. If somebody criticizes me or argues with me I just fold up and shrink into a corner, wishing I were invisible. Most of the time I'm just plain scared.

I wrote the role of "Kim" based on the contrasts I selected for Amy's words:

inferiority complex	explorer
shy	impish
nervous	energy
shrink	rage
invisible	flamboyant
scared	aggressive

Using the contrasting words, the character of "Kim" emerged.

I, Kim, have always been a tomboy. When I was little I could out-boy any boy on the block. I am still an explorer, a driver, a leader. I am aggressive in my approach to life. In fact I am downright flamboyant in both my personality and the way I dress. I enjoy attention and if others put me down, I think, "That's their problem, because I'm neat." When I get angry I not only express my anger openly, I rage. And once it's out I return quickly to my usual impish self.

I have too much energy to sit still for very long so I explore—new activities, new people, new roads, new thoughts, new goals. When I'm trying to make a decision on which way to jump next I get all the information I can, think over the pros and cons, then choose the one that feels right. If it turns out to be wrong for me I just give myself a hug and pick something else. I don't put myself down for making mistakes—how else can I learn? I don't just live life; I attack it. I have a lot of fun. And when I do feel down I repeat my favorite saying to myself over and over, "I am, therefore I'm worthwhile!" After all, who else is going to tell me that except myself!

Amy role-played going for a job interview as Kim. The group suggested that she act as if she were interviewing her prospective employer for the job, not the other way around. Once she had practiced in advance and had some idea of what she might say she did not feel so intimidated. She did go for several interviews subsequently. She told me later that she still did not really believe that she was worthwhile, but she kept repeating it to herself anyway. She said too that she felt less anxious thinking of herself as the interviewer. Eventually she found a job as a receptionist in an office. The last I heard from her was that she was next in line for office manager. Like Kim, Amy is now beginning to attack life rather than hide from it.

Alice B. came to my group on her caseworker's recommendation that she seek therapy to change the way she dealt with her son. Alice was twenty-two, very thin, and had a nervous laugh which often broke through her conversation, softening her usual frown. She told the group that she had never been happy. Her father was an alcoholic who had often beat her when she was a child. Her mother was also beaten, but despite her bitter complaints about her husband's behavior, she did nothing about it. Alice had married because she had gotten pregnant; it also seemed like a good excuse to leave home. She divorced her husband soon after her son was born. When she came to my group, she told me her problem was that when she got mad at her son she held in her anger as long as she could. When she could repress it no longer she usually beat him, hating herself for acting like her father. She wrote in her sketch:

> I am a <u>housewife</u> without a husband. I am also <u>lazy</u> and the world's worst procrastinator. I <u>know in my head</u> what to do and say that's right. But I just can't do all the things that I know should be done. I'm afraid that if I do something I might get yelled at for doing it wrong. I'm <u>nervous</u> most of the time and not really an outgoing person. I just sit around and let people run my life and tell me how to do things because if I speak up I'll start an argument. When I can't take it anymore I explode. I'm really <u>afraid</u> I'll turn out to be a <u>doormat</u> like my mother, or an angry drunk like my father, or both. I don't know how to change.

I chose the following words to contrast with Alice's sketch:

housewife	person
lazy	spontaneous
know in my head	assert my feelings

nervous	engrossed
afraid	assertive
doormat	free spirit

Then I wrote the role of "Tracy."

> My name is Tracy. I am what some might call a free spirit. I do not try to fit into categories. Although I could label myself—woman, mother, housewife—I prefer to think of myself as a person with the potential for being anything or anyone I choose. Sometimes when I find myself in new situations or with strangers I feel nervous but I usually become engrossed in the moment and forget myself. I am spontaneous in what I do. If I feel like running, I run; if I feel like wearing old tennis shoes to a formal gathering, I wear them. I like people but I know that not all people will like me so I don't worry about it if they don't. I am usually friendly but if I don't like what someone is saying or doing I'll tell them about it at once; I can be unfriendly at those times. If the other person doesn't like me then I don't try to be "nice" and apologize. I just stay with my own feelings and try to express them in as honest a way as possible. I am what you would call an assertive person.
>
> I assert my feelings with my own family but I know the difference between feelings and actions. When my kid bugs me I may yell at him, "I'm so angry at you I feel like hitting you," but I don't hit him. I may beat a pillow or stomp on the floor or yell a lot but I don't like to be hit so I don't hit anyone. And I don't mind it if he or anyone else gets angry with me. I figure others have as much right to their anger as I do. If my kid screams at me that he's angry or he hates me, I know that he'll feel better about me in a few minutes and then we can hug and make up. I also know that if I didn't let him express his anger at me he would stay angry and I don't want that. I'd rather have us all yelling out our feelings and getting them out and feeling good about each other than holding them in and carrying grudges for months. Ours is a loud and open relationship, painful at times but beautiful at others. And I want it to stay that way.

Alice came to group meetings for almost a year. During that time she stopped beating her son and started feeling more positive about herself. Her father died just before she quit the group, so she moved out of town to take care of his affairs. Several months later she called me up and told me how well she had taken care of not only the funeral arrangements and her father's property, but her mother (who had gone to pieces for several months) and her own boy as well. Alice had changed from a nonassertive person who let other people run her life to an individual who was capable of taking care of herself. She had gained some weight and dropped her nervous laugh. She said she felt confident of herself for the first time and was enjoying her new life. She even had a boyfriend and for once was not letting him or anyone else walk all over her. Alice sounded like she had truly become an assertive, open, feeling individual.

Martha S. found out about my group from a friend in her club for overeaters. She came into the group to work on her marital problems first, and her weight problem second. She told the group that after twenty years of marriage she was considering divorce. She said her husband bored her. Though they rarely fought, there was a wall of silence between them. She considered her husband cold and unfeeling but knew he was capable of exploding in anger. Rather than risk his anger she withdrew. She said she was tired of doing that and was at the point of calling it quits. I asked her to stay with the marriage until she had worked out enough of her own problems in therapy to be able to make a decision based on the realities of her situation, not just her fantasies of it. She agreed to do that. She wrote the following character sketch:

> I do not like myself, nor my husband. I feel frustrated most of the time—with me, with him, with my life. I'm bored and depressed. I'm unhappy and have no purpose to my life. I'm lonely, have no friends, and usually can't think of one thing to do to relieve my boredom except eat. And I hate myself for eating. But what else can I do? My life is empty and I'm empty inside. When I stuff myself with food I feel full for a short time but it doesn't last long. My doctor tells me to use will power to lose weight but I don't have any. I know all my fat is bad for my heart but somehow I'm powerless to stop eating. The more I eat the more I dislike myself. My parents disliked me, my husband dislikes me, so what else is new? I can't see any way out. I guess I'll be fat all my life.

I wrote the role of "Sheri," using the following key words to counter Martha's sketch:

bored	fascinated
depressed	absorbed
unhappy	wide-eyed
lonely	enjoying life
eating	feeling
empty	overflowing

Martha agreed that she would try to act out this role for a period of one month, keeping these attributes in mind.

I am Sheri. I am fascinated by what happens in life around me. Some people call me childlike because I walk around wide-eyed with the wonder of it all. I sometimes feel as if I had just emerged, a beautiful butterfly, from my enwrapping chrysalis into a world of joyful splendor. I see beauty in the simplest of things. I see colors in a soap bubble, a shine in my furniture as I polish it, the form of a leaf on a tree. I get pleasure from the touch of fur or velvet or stone or the skin of a friend's hand. I hear melody in a bird song or a child's voice. I see ugliness too and feel it with a sense of sadness. My secret for enjoying life is feeling it. I ingest it and it fills me to overflowing. I eat in the same way, absorbing my food for the taste and texture of each bite I take. I do not eat to fill my belly but my soul and I find I eat less than I used to—what need have I for food when I am filled with life?

I love people too and am as absorbed in them as in the rest of my life. Not that I'm Goody Two-Shoes with them. I let them know what I'm feeling when I'm feeling it and some people don't like that a bit. That's too bad if they don't; I'm not going to get an ulcer just because they choose to. And if they don't want to be around me when I'm throwing a tantrum, I don't let it bother me. Because I'm not only a neat person—I'm great, I'm super okay, I'm fantastic! And my life is super fantastic too.

Martha started losing weight with the help of her new role. I had suggested she put signs on her refrigerator and cupboard doors saying "I choose not to eat." She said that she had no will power to stop eating but realized for the first time that she had the power of choice. She also became very active in her club and started making new friends. Soon she found her life filled with people and things to do. She became less depressed, more energetic, and much more content with her daily routine. Her new self-image did not help her marriage, however. She put a lot of effort into improving the relationship; she even planned a week's vacation for the two of them in Hawaii. Her husband would still not let down his guard. The more open and outgoing she became, the more he seemed to resent it. Although he had often complained about her fatness in the past, he started urging her to eat more, commenting that she was easier to live with when she was fat. He particularly did not like her expressing her feelings. The straighter she was with her feelings, the more closed off he became. Finally he left her. She was sad about this for several weeks, but she realized the only way she could keep him was to go back to being her old withdrawn fat self. That she was unwilling to do. So she cried a lot but refused to beg him to come back. The last I heard from Martha was that she had gotten a divorce, had sold her house and moved into a modern apartment, and was even more active in clubwork. Her husband, she told me, had moved in with another woman—a motherly homebody who was very overweight.

I spoke earlier in this book about Darren S., who had learned since childhood to act the part of a hermit. Darren feared to communicate with others in any way. He was afraid to talk to other people, to meet their gaze, or to touch them physically. I remember patting him on the shoulder once; he jumped as if I had burned him. He was going to college during the year and a half he was in my group. He maintained a B average, worked hard, and had few problems with either tests or term papers. But he did nothing besides school work. He had no friends. He described his life on campus as a kind of ghostlike existence—floating through groups of students on his way to class, standing in crowds without touching or speaking to anyone, never speaking unless he was directly called on by an instructor. He was there in body but his inner self was split off and detached.

The one means of communication he permitted himself was through writing. He willingly wrote the following character sketch:

> I believe that <u>shyness</u> is probably the central trait of my character. I always wait for the other person to say the first word and carry the conversation. I am <u>afraid</u> I will say the wrong thing or that I have nothing to say that anyone else would be interested in hearing. I feel that I am <u>bothering</u> someone by talking to them. Since I desire to

avoid disagreements or conflicts, by keeping quiet I can avoid trouble. I try to avoid revealing myself to others by avoiding people and situations where conversation is expected. I feel different from other people my age because I do not seem to have similar interests and this perhaps contributes to a lack of topics to base a conversation upon.

I chose the following substitutions to counter Darren's words:

shyness	magnetism
afraid	excited
bothering	accepting
quiet	open
avoiding people	meeting people
different	special

I wrote a new role for Darren, which I called "Mark."

I, Mark, am a magnetic man and I know it. I enjoy meeting people and feel that they are attracted to me. Not that I rely on my magnetism alone in my interactions with others. I contribute freely to the conversation, willingly share where I'm at and am interested in hearing about the feelings and experiences of others. I used to worry about saying something dumb and hurting others' feelings so I didn't talk much. But then I decided that if I do that and somebody feels hurt, they've got a right to tell me about it and I'll accept it. If they don't tell me about it, hey, that's not my problem. That's theirs. Because I am an accepting guy. I accept others just as I accept myself. I'm not such a fantastic conversationalist, but I am a great listener and I find that others listen more to me because of it.

Sometimes I really feel excited when I start to talk to someone. My heart pounds, I feel shaky, my mouth gets dry and hands sweat. I used to think I was scared so I hated to meet anyone new. Then I decided to change the word "scared" to "excited" and I no longer dread meeting new people. I still feel shaky and sweaty but I just let myself be that way. As soon as I get going in the conversation those feelings go away and I find my sense of enjoyment coming back. I believe I am a special individual and others are special too. I have a right to my opinions and feelings and others have a right to theirs. If we differ, it's not that we argue; it's that we learn something from each other. And the more open I can stay with others, the more open they will be with me and the more I will gain from them. People are special and individual and usually just neat. And so am I.

Darren slowly began to change. He began to initiate conversations with other students on campus, even though he still thought he had nothing to say. As Mark, he role-played speaking to strangers and found that he could always talk about one common interest—classes. Eventually he took the risk of joining a club. That too gave him a new topic for conversation. I became aware that he was truly changing when he began to meet my eyes during group sessions instead of keeping his gaze lowered. And when he told the group one night that he was angry at them and me in particular, I clapped. "Good for you, Darren," I said. "You're really getting it on!" Hopefully, with Mark's help, he still is.

Our emotional problems stem from our original decisions to adapt to our parents' programming in some way and split off from our real, feeling selves. The purpose of any kind of therapy, therefore, should be to reunite our feeling selves with our cognitive, intellectual selves. If we integrate our selves we can experience our feelings in response to whatever is happening around us, without having to deny our feelings or suppress them in controlled rigidity.

Although the preceding examples of roles were written for different people and vary in character traits, all have certain commonalities. They all stress open expression of feelings, staying in the here and now, and *not* taking responsibility for the feelings of others. Some allow the role-player to brag about himself constructively; others focus on specific behaviors such as initiating conversation, conquering shyness, relieving boredom or getting out of depression. They are all written with the intent of reuniting the body with the senses, of allowing the role-player to trade suppression for expression.

All of the people of whom I have written have practiced their new roles and acted out situations in groups. I believe that it is easier to gain a concept of a new way of behavior by practicing beforehand in a supportive group. You can, however, do this on your own by practicing with strangers or with your family without revealing your purpose. You may want to keep a running written account to give yourself feedback on what you feel and on some of the life situations you encounter. You may even find that the behavior of others around you changes as a result of your new role. Write down your feelings about them too; eventually you may want to tell those close to you what you are doing. You do not have to reveal your new role; that is your choice. But if you want open, intimate relationships you will probably choose to share your feelings, since others around you may be confused by your changes.

When you start behaving in a different way according to your new role, you may start to gain things that you have always wanted in life—material possessions, careers, friends, interests. Some of your inner feelings will change accordingly. You will undoubtedly acquire a new sense of self-respect and a more positive self-image. The more you assert your feelings, the easier it will become; assertiveness, like anything else, improves with practice.

I do not propose that role therapy can be a panacea for all your problems. Certainly you can change by using this method, and certainly it will not be easy. It may take long, painful work on your part. And even if you do work for your own growth and achieve some changes in your life, you may still find yourself feeling bad, unable to alter certain deep-seated feelings of fear, hurt, despair, terror, self-destructiveness, or panic.

Suppose you do get everything you've ever dreamed of—a new job, money, prestige, friends, a lover—and then one night you wake up sweating in fear, panicked by you know not what. If these archaic feelings upset your life too much, you will need to consider working in greater depth on your feelings. You can change your behavior somewhat by using role therapy and gain certain tangible things. You may even be able to change some of your feelings. You may *not* be able to alter your deep core feelings.

Now that I've given you that word of caution, go ahead and write your character sketch, select a contrasting role, and start acting out your new role. Stay aware of your feelings as you role-play your new Self; let your feelings tell you if your new image fits comfortably or if you need to discard it. Find the reality of your own body. Take off your mask. You might discover that you like the person underneath.

The marriage myth

*Changing our expectations
may enable us
to find fulfillment and
have a satisfying relationship.*

The "myth of marriage" in our American culture teaches us the fairy tale of the sleeping princess and Prince Charming—"and he kissed her and she awoke from her long sleep. Then he picked her up in his arms and carried her off to his castle and they lived happily ever after." A recent magazine ad with a view toward women's lib changes this to "and *he* lived happily ever after." Nonetheless, thousands of people marry, expecting that marriage should bring happiness. When they find that happiness doesn't automatically come with the issuance of the marriage certificate, they divorce in ever increasing numbers. Did I hear on the news the other day that one out of every two marriages today is ending in divorce? It doesn't surprise me. What else can happen to a nation committed to the myth of marital "happiness"?

I use the word "myth" not because I believe happiness is unattainable but because I believe marital happiness, as pictured idealistically by the great majority of Americans, is an illusive and destructive fantasy. The great majority of us have been taught to believe that such happiness means constant harmony, peace and quiet, a calm and pleasant relationship—always. After all, the fairy tale promises, "happily *ever* after." So the goal of partners in marriage is to live happily; they each want the other to smile and be pleasant, and if one feels bad the other may say (as I have heard so many people express it), "Why can't you just be happy?"

Certainly moments of happiness can be attained, enjoyed, and cherished in memory until the next moment of happiness comes. But for happiness to last and last and last—ever after—is like taking a deep breath and holding it forever—or listening to the same overture forever—or remaining at the peak of your climax forever or laughing forever. Perhaps the fairy tale could be changed to say, "and they lived happily *sometimes* after." The meaning would be more precise even if the phrase were not quite so poetic. No happiness, no feeling, can be held forever. Between moments of happiness come moments of other feelings: anger, sadness, grief, fear, excitement, elation, and despair. And just as no one feeling can be constant, no marriage can be all placid; no relationship can be all smooth. If it always appears smooth on the surface there is no doubt trouble underneath. I have heard it said that those who cannot fight cannot love. In my experience, this has proven to be true. Those who do not express their angry feelings to each other invariably build up so much resentment that they no longer feel like loving each other in any way.

Jeanne and Mac M. had been married for over thirty years. They tried hard to make each other happy. To her this had meant being pleasant, keeping the house in order, making the children behave when he was home, and waiting on him. To him, this meant bringing home the paycheck, never expressing his negative feelings, doing what he thought she wanted, and defending her against the children. When they came to me for therapy they both blamed each other for their unhappiness. She told me nothing she did was ever right with Mac, and when she tried to tell him what she felt he accused her of complaining. She said the children were afraid to talk to their father because all he did was criticize them. He said she never appreciated anything he did for her, he was tired of giving in to her demands, and she had turned the children against him. They both felt guilty because they were not happy.

"Mac wants me to smile and be pleasant no matter how bad I'm feeling," Jeanne said. "When I try to tell him what I'm really feeling he says I'm bitchy. I can't stand being happy twenty-four hours a day just to please him."

"All I want is a little pleasantness," Mac said. "She's on my back constantly—Do this, don't do that, gripe, gripe, gripe. Nothing I do ever satisfies her. I don't want to go on living like this. And I sure don't want to retire and have to live with it day in and day out."

As a consequence of their buried feelings and unexpressed resentments they both felt depressed, tense, and enervated. They had long since given up doing things together to have fun. Their activites centered around home and work. Sex was almost nonexistent in their relationship, and their hours together were continuous battles, either of words or of strained silence. Not only did they suffer from the tension, but their children too were unhappy. Jeanne wanted to get out of the house and find some work of her own. Mac wanted to retire. They had no reason to believe that they could change their relationship and do what they wanted to do. They existed on a daily treadmill, each wondering if it were possible to hang together, both as individuals and as a couple, until the next day.

My first task in helping them change their attitudes was to challenge their mutual expectation that they should make each other happy. I had a tough time convincing them because they both believed so strongly in that "should." Not only their parents but our entire culture had conspired to enforce that belief. When I stressed the importance of *not* taking responsibility for each other's feelings, Jeanne asked, "Isn't it true that I am my brother's keeper?'

"Not in this sense," I replied. "You may find yourself responsible in part for your brother's welfare in the tangible sense of offering him food, money, and shelter. You can empathize with his feelings, listen to his problems, and cry with him in his grief. But you are not responsible for your brother's feelings. You simply do not have the power to make him feel. His feelings are his own."

"I can't accept it when you say he feels nothing because of what I do," she said.

"I didn't say that," I replied. "Certainly feelings are transmitted and can be caught like the common cold. But, like the cold, you have to be susceptible; in a sense you choose to catch it. You choose to catch feelings too, even though you may not like them. No one can *make* you feel, just as you cannot *make* another person feel. For example, let's say you go outside on a beautiful spring day feeling good and the first man you meet swears at you. You can feel a variety of feelings. Your initial response will probably be a moment of anger because he swore at you; in a sense he invaded your personal territory. You may get madder because you think he "should not" have sworn at you, or you may tune him out and ignore him because you've heard him swear so many times before. You may feel hurt because you think he must be right and you deserve to be sworn at. You may even feel happy because you aren't married to him and his problems. But he is not *making* you feel any of these things. He is only acting as the catalyst for your feelings."

"Are you saying I have a choice of feelings?" Jeanne asked.

"To a certain extent," I said. "You feel something initially because you respond to an event, but your response is your own and your choice of what to do with it is your own. One person might express her anger and feel elated, another might get depressed because he did not express his anger outright, another might feel even more hurt because she thinks no one loves her, and the last might chuckle all the way to work, thinking how lucky he is not to have to live with a person like that."

"You mean I can't make anyone feel good or bad?" Jeanne asked.

"Not really," I said. "Nor can anyone make you feel good or bad. You respond to events with appropriate feelings, but what you do with those feelings is up to you—your choice, your decision.

"Okay," Jeanne said. "I'll accept your idea that I can't make Mac happy by what I do, but I'll tell you, I can sure make him mad."

"How do you do that?" I asked.

"Like this morning, when he complained that I was going around with a sour face. I exploded. I told him what I felt, but good, and really made him mad. In fact he got so mad he threw a plate at me; I was afraid he was going to hurt me so I shut up. I'm still mad at him."

"What did you tell him?" I asked.

"I told him he was an s.o.b. and a lousy husband and if he didn't like the expression on my face, he could just pack his bags and get out," she said.

I sighed. One of the hardest tasks I have had as a teacher of personal growth and assertiveness is to teach people how to convey their feelings to others. As a nation, we are not used to dealing with our feelings. We are not taught how to recognize them, accept them, or express them to those around us. We mistake aggressiveness for assertiveness and wonder why others respond to us with so much anger. We dwell in our fantasies and believe we are responding with our senses. We give people our opinions and believe we are telling them what we feel. There is a world of difference between "I think" and "I feel." Once you can differentiate between expressing your opinions and expressing your feelings you will appreciate the great distance between the two.

Telling someone your opinion of him or her, as Jeanne did, is *not* expressing your feelings. When you tell others where to go, call them names, define them or give them commands, you are being aggressive; you are not telling him what you feel. Not that you need to put yourself down for being aggressive once in a while; we all act aggressively at times. But when you use aggressive language and behavior continually, others will usually respond to you with aggression. Sure, you will feel better if you're verbally aggressive than if you repress your bad feelings entirely; others may not. But you can communicate much more effectively and get more positive responses from others when you express your feelings directly, which is being assertive. Telling someone what you feel is describing to someone else what is happening in your own body. Others will more often than not respond with warmth when you tell them what you are feeling. They may even express surprise. "Why, I didn't know you felt like that" is a typical response.

Some people attempt to express their feelings and still convey opinions. When you say, "I feel that . . . ," it expresses an opinion, not a feeling. For example, "I feel that you are angry" is an opinion, or an observation about the other person, not an expression of your own feeling. If you were to express your feeling, you might say, "I'm feeling scared because I think you're angry." You need to listen to yourself and to choose your words carefully when you are starting to assert yourself. Some of the people in my classes have accused me of making them into "conversational idiots." After my class they have to stop and think about what they are going to say before they speak. Their conversations become stilted and full of pauses. So be it. It gets easier with practice.

I remember one of my class members once role-playing a scene with her boyfriend. She was trying to tell him what she felt and having great difficulty. At first she used a very aggressive approach, sure to escalate his aggression. She said, "You put me down when you said what you did. You're always doing that to me. You're a bastard." I told her that that was not really expressing her feeling and asked her to try the scene again, this time using "feeling language." So she role-played the last part of it again, ending up with "You're always doing that. I feel you're a bastard." Somehow, that still did not compute!

When Jeanne began to tell Mac what she was feeling in an assertive manner, rather than the aggressive style she had used in the past, he responded with less anger. Mac also learned to communicate his feelings openly to her. Mac's problems in the relationship had centered around the fact that he held in all his negative feelings up to a point. When he reached the "boiling" point he exploded, threw things around, and yelled. Once he tried to run Jeanne down with the car in their garage. Luckily, she jumped out of his way and was not hurt. Jeanne used to complain about Mac, "He has such a quick temper!" I told them both that Mac actually had a slow temper, explaining that he held in his feelings until he exploded. Through therapy, Mac learned to have a quicker temper, to express his irritation when he first felt it.

He also learned to accept Jeanne's negative feelings instead of expecting her to be happy all the time. When he dropped that unrealistic expectation he found that he felt irritated at her much less. She was less resentful because she didn't have to put up such a happy front. They both began to feel a great deal better about each other. They even became—to their amazement—happier. The last time I spoke to Jeanne and Mac they were still married. Jeanne decided she really did not want to get a job. She realized she was happiest working in her own home. And Mac was looking forward without trepidation to retirement.

Some of my clients have fallen into another trap in their marriages—the trap of expecting one's spouse to represent some ideal. I remember Louise A. saying at our first session, "I feel frustrated and disappointed in my marriage and in my husband. We've been married eighteen years, have three lovely children and a beautiful home, but it's become meaningless. I can't rely on Will anymore for anything. He won't do anything around the house; he puts off all the jobs he says he'll do; he won't discipline the children and when I want to talk to him about it he makes some silly joke."

"What do you expect from him?" I asked.

"I expect him to act like a man and a father," she said.

"What is that?" I asked.

"What do you mean, what is that," she said angrily.

"I don't know what expectations you have in your head or what your image of a man and a father is. I'd like to hear you define your terms."

"A man should be strong enough to be the head of the household, assume responsibility for his family, be leaned on without falling over, make decisions. A father should spend time with his children and discipline them when they don't behave. Will doesn't do any of these. I have to. He's not a man at all; he's a worm."

"You sound very angry," I said.

"You bet I'm angry," she said. "I'm doing everything that he should be doing and I don't know how to get him to take over his responsibilities. I've tried everything I know how. I think I'm going to have to divorce Will to wake him up. Do you have any suggestions?"

"The first thing to do is to stop expecting," I told her.

"I don't understand," she said.

"Stop expecting him to be a man and a father. Those are ideals that you have in your own head based on your own beliefs. Stop expecting him to do what you want him to do and accept him as he is. The more you expect of him the more he will rebel against your expectations. Stop expecting, period."

"If I can't expect anything of him, then what am I married for?" she asked.

"That's up to you to decide," I said. "But if you don't accept your husband as he is right now, you won't be married for long."

We battled over her expectations for several sessions before she began to accept my reasoning. She discovered that her husband was rebelling against her expectations indirectly but very effectively. He procrastinated, he forgot and he joked. There was little she could say to him when he responded to her queries, "Oh, I'm sorry about that. I just forgot." When she stopped expecting him to live up to her ideas on how he should behave, he began to do things on his own initiative. She also discovered that her conception of what Will should be was based on her feelings about her father. She had always been afraid of her father and was still angry at him. She had chosen Will because he was unlike her father; he had been impulsive, devilish and quick at repartee when they married. Yet she expected her husband should be "strong," authoritative, and a worker around the home—just like her father. When Louise began to accept Will as a person in his own right, a person who had positive attributes as well as faults, she stopped expecting him to live up to her fantasized ideal.

I know, of course, that there are some expectations that people inevitably have of each other. You expect your partner to behave in certain ways that you have mutually agreed upon—to get up and go to work, to take the children to the doctor, to maintain the cars, to buy food, or whatever. If two people in a relationship have learned what each can expect from the other and then one starts behaving very differently, it certainly may be cause for alarm. Suppose one of the two suddenly stops working and refuses to contribute to the family income, or leaves for no apparent reason, or turns off sexually, or suddenly decides not to do any of the housework. Some specific expectations, based on prior knowledge of one's partner's habits and behavior, are unavoidable. But vague expectations based on one's own belief system are extremely destructive to a relationship.

I have often suggested to couples that they check out their expectations by each writing down a list of "shoulds." You might try this too. Write down all the expectations you have of your spouse. Ask your spouse to do the same. When you have your "Should Lists" completed, compare them and discuss each "should" in detail. If you do not mutually agree on a "should," check its validity. Is it real and appropriate to your relationship? If it is not, either drop it entirely or make it more specific. For example, Louise's Should List contained many unreal expectations: 1) Will should be a man, 2) Will should be a good father, 3) Will should work around the house. These were vague and undefined. Will simply could not agree to conform to Louise's generalized ideal, since he had no clear idea of what it was. So she dropped the generalities and they worked on specifics. She changed number 1 to "Will should express his anger rather than pout." Will agreed with that, so they worked on giving him permission to express his feelings directly. Number 2 became "Will should tell the children what he wants them to do rather than criticize them for being lazy." Will agreed with that too. Number 3 was changed to "Will should repair the roof, maintain the lawn and make repairs in the house as needed." Will did not agree with the first point but he did agree to let Louise hire someone to make the repairs. He agreed to the other points. They both discovered that when they brought their expectations down to specifics they could understand what the other was talking about and make decisions based on realities rather than fantasies.

Will himself had been confused by an expectation of his own, that he should try to please his wife and that Louise should be pleased by what he did. He had tried hard throughout their marriage to do just that and he usually ended up displeasing her. When he tried to please her several things happened. First, he usually did things for her that he would have liked her to do for him; she was not pleased. Second, he resented "having" to put her pleasure before his own, so he was quick to become angry when she did not appreciate what he did. Third, when she told him she did not like what he did he either exploded in anger or sank into a hurt silence that might last for days.

Typical of this pattern were the times he had tried to please her on special holidays by bringing her breakfast in bed. Each time he did this Louise would say, "Please don't bring me breakfast in bed again. I don't like to eat in bed; I feel awkward and I spill crumbs all over. I would rather get up and eat at the kitchen table." And Will would inevitably respond, "But dear, I'm only trying to please you." This had been going on for eighteen years.

When I asked him what he thought when she expressed her dissatisfaction with eating breakfast in bed he said, "Oh, I know she doesn't mean it. She's only being nice and trying to save me the time and trouble of fixing breakfast."

"What if she does mean it?" I asked.

"I guess I would have wasted a lot of effort," he said.

"By doing something for her that would have pleased you!" I said.

"Sure," he agreed. "I'd love to have breakfast in bed but Louise likes to sleep in. She doesn't cook breakfast."

"Look," I said. "How about reversing your thinking. Instead

of trying to please her, tell her what you would like her to do to please you! Think of pleasing yourself first."

"But that's selfish," Will said.

"Yes, it is," I agreed. "But think of all the breakfasts in bed you might have gotten all these years. Being selfish is okay in the sense that you need to please yourself first. Then you can give to others without resentment. There's a difference between 'selfish' and 'self-centered.' I think of 'selfish' in a positive sense because you need to be concerned about yourself. If you aren't concerned about yourself nobody else will be either. You'll find those around you expecting more of you the more you give to them and you will end up feeling very martyred. 'Selfish,' in my thinking, is the opposite of 'martyr.' On the other hand, I think of 'self-centered' in a negative sense because you cannot perceive others if you are occupied only with yourself. And if you cannot perceive others you will never be able to communicate with them intimately. You will be locked into your own shell."

"If I were selfish Louise wouldn't like it," Will said.

"How do you know?" I asked. "Give her a chance to be selfish too. Ask her what she wants you to do to please her. If each of you is concerned first about yourselves and what feels good for you, you won't feel so resentful about giving to the other person. You will be sharing out of a sense of fullness rather than straining to please her and then feeling cheated yourself."

"I'll think about it," Will said.

"Good enough," I said. "What have you got to lose? Trying to please hasn't worked in eighteen years. Maybe this will."

Louise was jubilant when Will told her about our conversation. She called me up to tell me about it.

"You finally got through to him," she said. "All these years when I've told him I didn't like his little surprises he simply didn't believe me. Now he's asking me what I want instead of thinking he can read my mind."

"How are you going to manage getting up to fix him breakfast in bed?" I asked.

"I'll manage," she said. "I'll get it ready the night before. And it won't hurt at all. I'll trade every breakfast in bed on holidays for something that *I* want. The first thing I want is a trip to Reno."

"Some trade," I said.

"You don't know what a sacrifice it is for me to get up first in the morning," she said. "But it will be worth it if I start getting what I want instead of what Will thinks I want. I might even manage going to some of his baseball and hockey games in trade for his going someplace with me."

Will and Louise are still together; they have long since abandoned their thoughts of divorce. Their marriage is not perfect but they are each getting more of what they want out of it instead of straining to give to each other. They do not hesitate to communicate their feelings and their wants openly. They feel better about themselves and about each other. Each has learned to accept each other as he or she is, not as he or she should be. And they have learned to relinquish control.

Control is really what marital battles are all about—who is going to control whom. When you have some preconceived expectation of your partner in your mind you are trying to control. If your partner rebels—in such a situation most people will—the battle is on! When you give up your expectation, however, you give up your control. Your partner then has no reason to rebel, consequently you have less to fight about. You allow each other to Be. You respond to each other as you feel—neither trying to ensure that the other will act a certain way, just responding to how the other person does act.

When I think of control, I often refer to Cornelis Bakker's theories on the management of territories in human relationships. His ideas help me clarify what is going on in a conflict. People are often involved in conflicts concerning what Bakker calls "action territory"—any area in a relationship that involves doing something such as tasks or jobs. Usually one wants to give action territory away. When a couple is arguing over who does the dishes or who takes out the garbage they are fighting over action territory, trying to get the other person to take over the job. An element of control goes with each task. Have you ever said to someone, "I'd like you to do this," and implied, "my way!"? And, have you heard in return, "Well, if you feel that way about it, you can do it yourself"? (I have.) If you try to give away a task and still keep control of it, you will find that it is almost impossible to get rid of. Bakker states, "To the extent that a person feels coerced to take care of a certain territory, he does not experience it as his own."* You can negotiate on which tasks or jobs you wish to retain, but if you want to get rid of the job, give away your control along with it.

Louise discovered that she could negotiate with Will on certain tasks, just as they had learned to trade off what each wanted to get from the other. But she also found out the basic reason why Will had been unwilling to do tasks before. She had wanted him to do things her way. For example, she wanted Will to help out with the dishes but she insisted he scrape the dishes and put them in the dishwasher the same way she did. When he did it his way she criticized him for not doing it "right." Consequently he procrastinated so often she had quit asking him, while still resenting him for not helping out. It was the same for other tasks she wanted him to do around the house. When she stopped telling him to do things her way and allowed him to do the tasks in his own way, he was much more willing to help out.

Then, instead of criticizing him for not doing a job "right," as she had done in the past, she deliberately picked something she could compliment him about. Or maybe she just said, "Thank you." When she gave him praise and encouragement for what he did instead of criticism for what he did not do, she found Will much more willing to help out around the house. She was not always satisfied with the results but she realized that, if she tried to retain control of what he did, she would end up with the same territory she had before. So again she dropped her expectations of how he should do things and tried to accept what he did do.

Negotiating about disciplining the children was more difficult, because Louise and Will both had strong ideas on this. Their three children had equally strong ideas. I asked them as a family to each write out a "Should List," including what each expected for themselves and from the others. Then I suggested they sit down in a family council and discuss their lists. When they did this they found that they could make many of their generalized "shoulds" more specific and appropriate to the real situation. They did not arrive at any perfect solution. But they did find that they could understand

*Cornelis B. Bakker and Marianne K. Bakker-Rabdau, *No Trespassing, Explorations in Human Territoriality* (San Francisco, Chandler & Sharp Pub. Co. 1973), p. 26.

what each was thinking much more clearly and find certain points on which they could negotiate.

I much prefer Bakker's term "negotiation" to the word "compromise." To me, compromise means to give in. I feel a compromise as a defeat. But to me, negotiate means to bargain. I feel more equal about it. For example, my husband loves to fish; I do not. When he used to want me to go fishing with him continually, and I went, I became very resentful. I started inventing excuses to stay home. Then I decided to negotiate with him and I felt better. I told him I wanted him to go to dance classes with me. "Otherwise," I said, "I don't want to go fishing with you anymore." He agreed even though he did not really like to dance. He grumbled a lot before classes, but he went. I figured that he was entitled to grumble as long as he stuck to our agreement. A bargain is a bargain. And I went fishing with him (even though I grumbled).

Think of the word "control," and you might be able to clarify what is happening in your own relationships. You may quickly discover why you are meeting with rebellion or sheer hostility on the part of your children or mate. For example, if you are still telling your teenager son, "Hurry up, you're going to be late for school," you are trying to control him. Naturally, he rebels by sleeping longer, you get angrier, he gets hostile and you are both upset. Give him back his territory. Buy him an alarm clock and let him be late a few times. It is his problem, not yours. If he cannot handle this territory by now he never will.

You can even hand over a certain amount of control to little children. I remember when my little girl started preschool I would try to pick out her clothes in the mornings. After a few deadlocked fights I gave her control of that territory. She then picked out what she wanted to wear, within limits. I would not let her go to school in winter wearing a bikini. But she could wear a dress or pants suit, and any color she chose. She picked out some outfits that were pretty fantastic. But gradually, with feedback from other children, she learned what was appropriate to wear and what was not. We now have few hassles over the issue because I have few expectations. And she seldom has reason to rebel about clothes.

Children are often heavily controlled by parents in areas related to food—what foods to eat, when to eat, how to eat. I have had numerous clients who remembered having had stomachaches as children regularly at dinnertime, or who still cannot eat certain foods, or who developed ulcers, all because their parents had control of mealtimes. One client was terrified of sitting down to a formal dinner with other people. She believed she would throw up, as she had done so often as a child. Another client told me she hated to sit at a table because she had so many bad memories of her father insisting she sit there until he finished eating. So now she stands at a counter to eat or sits on the floor.

The fewer expectations you have of your children's eating habits, the easier it will be on everyone concerned. Certainly, keep nutritious food on hand and put a limit on junk food and snacks. It's okay to establish a few rules. But keep them few. If you have many expectations of your children about food and mealtimes they may have lifelong problems related to food. They will make your expectations into their own. Unless they learn to stop listening to your messages in their heads, they will forever control themselves according to your expectations.

Elizabeth O. was controlled by her own self-image. Her expectation of herself was that she should be a good wife, a good mother, a competent hostess, and a lady. She had fulfilled some of these expectations to her own satisfaction. She was an excellent hostess. She knocked herself out for her girls, thereby convincing herself she was a good mother in the conventional sense of the term. But she found that being both a good wife and a lady created an insoluble problem. If she was a lady she could not "let herself go" in the bedroom; therefore she could not be a good wife. Her solution, for fifteen years of marriage, was to fake it. She pretended to enjoy making love but had never once experienced orgasm.

"I guess I'm just frigid," she told me.

"I don't believe that," I said. "Maybe in a rare case there might be a physiological inability to achieve orgasm, but for the great majority of people sexual problems are simply problems with feelings in general. If you aren't in touch with your feelings in other areas, how can you allow yourself to experience sexy feelings?"

"I do feel in other areas," she said.

"What do you feel?" I asked.

"I feel happy, I feel sad, I feel frustrated and lonely—lots of different feelings," she said.

"Do you ever feel excited? Do you get angry? Do you feel exultant and joyful?" I asked.

"Not very often," she said. "I experience some of those feelings at times but I keep them inside."

"How come?" I asked.

"I guess I've always been taught that ladies behave in certain ways," she said.

"Which ways?" I asked.

"Well, a lady should be gracious, kind, calm, able to maintain her poise no matter what, and not throw herself around. She should be, well, sedate."

"Wow," I said. "No wonder you won't allow yourself to feel sexy. How can you possibly have an orgasm if you calm yourself down the moment you start feeling excited?"

"I can't," she said.

And she was right. As long as she expected herself to behave like a lady she trapped herself into a self-image of a poised, unfeeling individual who would never let herself go. When she started to experience feelings of excitement during sex she would turn herself off, believing "ladies don't feel like that." She usually felt tense and frustrated and had a variety of pains—headaches, backaches, stomachaches—which were undoubtedly connected to her constant state of physiological stress. In Elizabeth's case the excuse "Not tonight, dear, I've got a headache" was indeed accompanied by a tangible pain in her head. And she experienced more and more physical complaints as the years went on. Her self-expectation that she act like a lady not only had a direct bearing on her "frigidity," but because of her physical ailments on other aspects of her life as well. She felt hopeless about ever achieving orgasm or changing her sexual behavior.

"Who laid the 'Behave like a lady' message on you?" I asked.

"I do," she said, "all the time."

"No, I mean originally," I said. "You don't give yourself 'shoulds.' You get them from your parents. Which parent expected you to be a lady?"

"Both, really," she said. "Father got very angry if I acted silly or tomboyish and told me about it at great length. And Mother is a lady. She would be very upset if I weren't. I see Mother in my head a lot and I act the way she acts. I've been taught that her way is the right way to behave."

"Then you need to stop listening to your father and stop mimicking your mother's behavior. Every time you hear your father's lectures, turn him off. Give yourself a permission message instead, like 'It's okay to feel' or 'It's okay if I feel sexy' or 'I don't have to be a lady anymore.' Anything that makes sense to you. And when you see your mother in your head, tell her to go away. Give yourself permission to act the way you want to act instead of following her example. In fact, you need to do more than just turn them off. You need to kill the parents in your head. Silence them forever. Only by doing that can you stop expecting yourself to behave in a certain, set way and learn to act according to the way you really feel."

"It's a big order, but I'll try it," she said. "I've been acting like a lady so long that it's become a habit and I'll really have to think about how I really do feel and what I really want. But I'll do it. I don't want to go on for the rest of my life the way I've gone on so far."

A week later she called me up with fantastic news. She had tried my suggestion and it worked. I was amazed because she had had only the one therapy session with me. She said that she had not felt able to kill the parents in her head so she decided to chloroform them instead. To put her resolution to the test she called her husband up at work one afternoon and asked him to come right home. She told him she had a surprise for him. When he got home she met him at the door in her negligee. Needless to say he was flabbergasted but managed to maintain his equilibrium enough to participate manfully in the activities that followed. They were both delighted with the results. Elizabeth turned off her parent messages: "What if the neighbors hear," "The children might come home any minute," "Ladies don't act this way," "People don't do it in the daylight," and all the rest. For the first time in her life she achieved an orgasm.

What is even more fantastic is that Elizabeth has had no problems attaining orgasm since. Once she knew how to chloroform the parents in her head she was able to shut them up every time and substitute permission messages like "It feels good to be sexy," "My body is okay," and "I like sex." She and her husband still have plenty of other problems in their relationship but, for the first time in all their years together, sex is not one of them. Elizabeth has no more expectations about her behavior when it comes to sexual feelings. She just takes sex as it comes, when it comes—and enjoys it.

People form marital relationships with a wide variety of expectations depending upon their childhood experiences and feelings about them, the parent messages they hear in their minds, and whether or not they've adapted to or rebelled against those messages. As children, we adjust to our family symbiotically in order to survive. When we grow up and leave home we look for other relationships in which we can continue to survive. Because we know no other we tend to look for relationships similar to the symbiotic bonds of childhood. So it is natural for those of us who have been abused as children to seek out relationships in which we will continue to be abused. It is equally natural for those of us who have been given adequate nurturing as children to seek partners who will continue to give us that nurturing. A relationship we develop may not be comfortable if it is based on a heavy and unfulfilled symbiotic need, but it may be somehow familiar in all its misery. If we leave such relationships without uncovering the source of our feelings, we may continue to find new relationships similar to those we have left behind.

Partners in symbiotic marital relationships often express the desire to change each other. In some cases the relationship may be based on one partner's wanting to "save" the other, for example, the woman who marries an alcoholic believing that he will be able to stop drinking with her love to strengthen him. This desire to change the other, expressed later as an expectation, has more to do with the parent than the mate. For children keep hoping that their controlling, demanding, or abusive parents will change into the loving, nurturing, permitting parents they want and need in order to mature. If children remain stuck in their symbioses, it is natural for them, as adults, to choose mates for the purpose of changing them. They will choose their spouses, not necessarily because they resemble the unchanged parents, but because their mates activate feelings in them similar to those their parent evoked. They will expect their partners to behave as they believe their parents should and when their expectations are not met, they will be hurt, angry, and resentful. If they divorce their mate and yet remain stuck in their symbioses, their tendency will be to seek out similar relationships in the future. Why? To continue trying to get the mate to give them the love they never got from their parents. Their useless struggles will not end until they quit trying to get that love that exists only in their fantasies—until they stop expecting.

For this reason I usually ask couples who come to me for therapy to make a contract not to divorce for a certain period of time. After this period they may have worked through and understood enough of their symbiotic needs to be able to make a rational decision about their relationship, based on their feelings in the here and now. Within limits, of course. Sometimes it is a sign of health to get out of a sick relationship as fast as possible, for instance, a relationship in which a husband continually beats his wife and refuses to stop. If a wife remains in a marriage in which she is physically abused by her husband, she is as much at fault as he is. She is getting some kind of payoff from the beatings, even if that payoff is a barrel full of bad feelings and put-downs.

Another restrictive expectation that many people have is that they become a "we" after marrying. In my thinking, attaining the status of "we" is a dubious distinction of the marriage ceremony. Before marriage a couple may maintain their separate identities, even when living together. They are not as pressured to take on constricting roles (good wife, mother, breadwinner, hard worker), nor live up to fantasized expectations. They have more freedom to be themselves. After marriage, however, the "We Trap" closes. Relatives, friends, and society in general all exert subtle pressures on the couple to conform to some idealistic norm. If they decide to remain childless (some are now calling that state "child-free"), to maintain certain premarital friendships, or to hold a portion of their lives apart from the "we," the couple may receive pressure from well-meaning people around them. The couple, as a "we," are expected, and expect, to live happily ever after. How is that possible as two separate individuals, two "I's" with feelings, thoughts, dreams, and aspirations of their own?

I do not view partners within a marriage as a "we." I see them as two separate "I's." If they insist on remaining a "we" the partners may feel increasing resentment towards each other. Two horses pulling a wagon form a "we." Neither can go his separate way. They are forced to plod along together, regardless of individual desires. Two marital partners need not be that limited. As "I's," they may agree to disagree, each respecting the other's right to have differing opinions. They may follow different courses of action. They may also recognize each other's feelings without taking responsibility for them. The danger of the "We Trap" is that both partners will negate their separateness and begin to cater and defer, trying to please the other. When that happens, the resentment begins to build, as it did with Louise and Will.

How much healthier it is for each partner to accept his or her own individuality and separateness, to regard the partnership as two people, two "I's"! Then they may have feelings, thoughts, and aspirations separate from each other. They may even choose to keep a certain separateness in their lives. They may go on separate vacations, maintain separate bank accounts, pursue separate hobbies, and have separate friends. Certainly they need to maintain a balance to ensure that they set enough time aside from their other pursuits to pay attention to each other. It's not the quantity of time they spend with each other that counts; it's the quality of their time together. But this balance, this quality time, can be achieved; it is the total happiness of the "we" that cannot.

I think of a "we" relationship that strives for constant happiness as a straight line. To me, that line does not represent happiness at all, but dullness, sameness, and boredom, along with resentment and depression. I think of the relationship of two "I's" as a curving line. This curved line represents to me change—feelings that change from day to day: joy, anger, excitement, grief, exultation, sadness —in short, the whole range of huamn emotions as the "I's" experience and express them. Two "I's" permit each other to feel whatever each is feeling when each is feeling it without restrictions, expectations or "shoulds." So the relationship changes daily according to what each partner is feeling at the time. It is far more stable than a relationship in which neither is permitted to feel and express those feelings. That rigid relationship is more likely to foster resentments and hostilities which will someday either explode outwardly in aggressive acts or implode inwardly in bodily ailments.

Other expectations affecting marital relationships concern the ambiguous word "love." People are taught to believe that the one who says "I love you" means well toward them. Actually the word "love" may have a variety of meanings. "I love you" might be more appropriately rephrased as "I need you to take care of me," "I need to take care of you," "I want to control you," "I want you to be mean to me," "I want to save you," or "I want to use you." If the words "I love you" actually mean that the speaker wishes to control you in some way, then it is not love that is being offered but hostility. Love means to allow the other person to be free to feel, be, and grow as an individual. Any expectation that personal freedom be restricted by love should rightly be examined with suspicion. Viewed in this light, the people who believe that they should form a "we" after marriage, with little or no freedom to pursue their "I" identities, are hostile toward each other. They are restricting each other's ability to grow as individuals and are perhaps setting the stage for lifelong marital battles.

Such restrictions, of course, may exist in one's own thought processes without being expected by one's partner. A woman in a class of mine told me about going for a walk with a friend she had just met. The next day, she said, she received a card from him professing his love.

"I can't trust that," she explained. "How can he fall in love with me after such a short time? I'm angry at him for sending me that card."

Her reaction seemed extreme to me.

"What does love mean to you?" I asked.

"I don't know, really," she said. "I've never thought about it."

We talked about her definition of the word, about what it had meant in her family when she was a child, and what it meant to her in her former marriage. Finally she was able to clarify what she meant by the word love.

"To me it means service," she said. "I was the oldest of five children and my mother died when I was twelve. I had to take care of the younger children while my father worked. I couldn't go out on dates or have fun because I was always too busy doing housework. I couldn't go to college because I was needed at home. When the kids finally grew up enough to take care of themselves I was able to leave home and get married. But that turned out to be the same thing. I served my husband and my own children. I had no interests of my own; everything I did was for them. Love has meant nothing to me but hard work and I'm scared of it. 'To love is to serve.' Boy, have I heard that one a lot!"

"So, when someone says, 'I love you,' it means that if you return his love you will have to give up your own life and interests and cater to his needs," I said.

"That's right," she said. "I've just started to find myself after being divorced for a year. I don't want to get roped into taking care of someone else again so soon."

"What if you could love someone and be loved in return without serving him, have love and be able to give it and still have your own life?" I asked.

"That might not be too shabby," she said.

We role-played a situation where her friend gave her a present as a further protestation of his love and she expressed to him her fears about accepting it. A week later I asked her if she had gained anything from our discussion and role-play. She reported that her friend had indeed brought her a gift. She had decided to accept it as a token of affection with no obligation attached. She had told her friend about her fear of love and they had had a long discussion about it.

"I feel very comfortable talking to him about this and I've learned a lot from him. We've talked about deeper feelings than I've ever discussed with anyone—man or woman. I don't know where the relationship will go. It may lead to marriage and it may not. I've decided to just take it as it comes and enjoy it. I'm no longer worried about it anymore—or about love." By dropping her expectation that love between a man and a woman meant that the woman was to serve her man forever, she was able to respond to her new friend with her present feelings rather than her past fantasies. She was also able to stop expending her energies through anxiety and start enjoying the here and now.

Loving is also confused with living together. They are commonly understood to be one and same thing. Actually, they are not. I think of loving and living together as two separate concepts. There are some people who love each other very much, but who would never want to live together. There are others who do not passionately love each other in the conventional sense of the term, but they live together very harmoniously. It is also possible to love some qualities in an individual, but not enough to want to set up housekeeping together. And it is possible to love more than one individual at one time but to decide not to establish more than one ongoing relationship. There are more kinds of love than there are lovers. But ongoing relationships are not based so much on some mysterious alchemy as on simple decisions. Do you have enough desire, respect, and trust for this person, and do you share enough intimacy to balance out your negative feelings? If the answer is "yes," then your decision may be that there is enough "love" to establish a living pattern with that person. If the answer is "no," your decision may be to love still but maintain your own apartment.

Becoming sexually involved with someone is also a decision and an action. Just because you feel sexually turned on by someone does *not* mean you must hop into bed with that person. Many people might turn you on, which is okay; it shows you're alive and well. But if you decide to have sex with those people, your marital relationship may suffer. I know of some people, however, who do not recognize the difference between feelings and acting out those feelings. They are afraid of having sexual feelings for or fantasies about anyone other than their mates. They have been taught that they're immoral, irresponsible, even wanton, if they feel turned on by anyone else. Instead of allowing themselves to experience their feelings, they guiltily turn themselves off, deadening themselves sexually even more than they already are. They don't realize that feelings are different than actions and they have a choice about taking their feelings home, acting them out or turning off.

Love, intimacy, and sexual feelings are simply feelings and do not have to be translated into actions. I believe we miss out on a whole lot of love and strokes by confusing feelings with sexual actions. Our idealized beliefs about monogamous relationships and our confusion about intimacy and love may keep us from attaining intimate friendships outside our home environment. Monogamy, to many of us, means never looking at, thinking about, or feeling anything for anyone other than our partners. If we believe this we may weigh our partners down by demanding that they fill us with love. When they, being human, cannot fill all our needs, we end up resenting them. So by turning ourselves off to our feelings for others we may be turning ourselves off to our partners as well.

Loving touch is okay; if you feel close to another person you may hug or kiss without deciding to go any further. I'm a hugger; I love to be hugged by people I care about. I get good, warm feelings from physical touch. I regret the years I distanced myself from people, in fear of physical contact. But no more; now I'm a firm believer in touching. I think big people need to be touched, caressed, stroked every bit as much as babies do. Yet because I hug and touch a person does not mean I have to act out any sexy feelings I may have. It's my decision. I may love, feel intimate, and touch many people yet choose to have sex only with my marital partner.

I know that I cannot have all my needs met by my husband and my child. I need friends to talk to, colleagues to discuss problems with, and some relatives to whom I can tell my feelings. I like to get strokes and feel competent in work that does not involve my family members. And sometimes I need to complain about my family to a good listener just to keep my perspective. I imagine that you are like me in this respect and need many people to relate to in depth, with intimacy and love. We no longer have extended families surrounding us to fill our needs for intimacy. We do not commonly live with grandparents, parents, children, uncles and aunts under the same roof. So we need to have intimates outside our immediate family, within our extended family of humankind.

With these thoughts on love I come back to the point with which I began this chapter. In our culture we expect to "fall in love and live happily ever after." I feel boxed in even writing these words. Somehow I am reminded of movies of the thirties, the big-band era, togetherness, suburbia, moonlight and roses, machismo, and romanticism. Yes, that's it. Loving and living together happily ever after is a notion that we Americans have been spoon-fed ever since the romanticism of the eighteenth century. I remember one line in Zane Grey's *Riders of the Purple Sage* that exemplifies my view of the romantic philosophy. The heroine and her cowboy hero had climbed to the rim of the cliff with the badmen hot on their heels. The pair had the choice of sealing themselves off from the world forever in the the valley in front of them or turning and facing their pursuers. They hesitated momentarily. Then the heroine hardened her jaw, thoughts of family, home and chastity put firmly behind her, and said, "Lassiter, roll the stone."* The rock rolled, it closed the opening, and they were forever alone.

Unfortunately, there are no perfect valleys. There is no per-

*Zane Grey, *Riders of the Purple Sage* (New York, Harper & Row, 1912), p. 280.

fect marriage. There is no ideal love. There is no forever. Reality means imperfection, upset, and change. The heroine and her lover are supposed to live together happily ever after in their sequestered valley. But I picture the little nuisances—the mosquitoes, droughts, and arguments, the lack of outside news, the colds, fever blisters, and petty hassles. I should imagine it wouldn't be too long before one of the two would be climbing the valley walls trying to find a pathway out.

I would love to say to you that if you only do such and such your relationships will be constant, life will be forever good, love will be always sweet. But I can't lie to you or to myself. A good relationship is viable, flexible, permitting of feelings, and open to change. It may last forever in its impermanence or it may end tomorrow. There are no guarantees. The only perfection is in the grave; there we are perfectly dead. On this side of the grave we know only the reality of change.

So the myth of the prince and princess and their romantic love is quite simply wrong. Any princess who sleeps until her prince comes is going to sleep a long, long time. Actually, I see women who are waiting for their heroes not as heroines but as victims waiting for someone to rescue them from their fates and to solve all their problems. They will probably find that hero; many American men have been trained by their romantic mothers to fit the role. But will any of these relationships be "happily ever after"? No. Too often the hero changes into the forest ogre who turns the princess into his very own workaday Cinderella.

Or, he may end up the victim. After he finds his sleeping beauty and kisses her awake she may turn into a screaming, complaining witch of a princess who orders him to get on his horse and put some food on the table. He may wish she'd go to sleep again but unfortunately, after you wake up a sleeping witch, she rarely shuts up. She is more likely to keep on screaming, until either the prince gets wise and leaves, or hooks his charger to a plowshare and high-tails it out to the fields where he can enjoy some peace and quiet.

Then the honeymoon is over. She, feeling powerless, sits among the cinders bewailing her fate, while he can work his way to an early heart attack, but peacefully. Each is equally responsible for remaining in a manipulative relationship. The victim is as responsible, sometimes even more, as the ogre or the witch. Each can express feelings and desires to the other person, each can threaten, beg, plead, scream, or cajole, but neither can *make* the other change. If he chooses to remain the forest ogre or she the screaming witch, the choices are two: either accept one's role and submit, or get out.

Either person may be the first to change. The princess may decide, if she has been a victim, to stand up, brush off her cinders, and climb over the wall. Or, the prince may get tired of working his horse to death for some screaming witch and simply quit. Either may go off to find some wide-awake prince or princess who is not a romantic. Both may, of course, pick a new mate exactly like the old one; old habits are tough to break.

But these habits *can* be broken. People *can* drop their manipulations and, through awareness, choose to change.

6

Heroes and hero-makers

*With awareness
of what we are doing,
manipulation can be useful
in a relationship.*

We have come to think of the word "manipulate" in a negative sense, as if one who manipulates *deliberately* intends to do harm. I have started thinking of it in a different sense, however, because I realize that at times each of us manipulates others around us. And, I realize that we do this, not usually out of deliberate intent, but out of lifelong habits and fears, both past and present.

I have read many books about the various kinds of manipulations people use, the games they play, and with each book I've gotten the same message—SHAME!—if you are a manipulator, you're bad! Perhaps that tiny part of me with remaining feelings of worthlessness picks up on this message, but oh my, have I ever picked it up! I've read each book like a second-year medical student looking for a disease. Who me? I do that? How terrible, and how do I get rid of it?

Well, someplace along the path of growth I said, Stop! I admit that I do manipulate. But nobody, no matter how important, okay, together or perfect relates to others totally without manipulation. Nobody can be intimate, in the sense of being totally open to others, always and with everybody. And would we even want to be? We may not care to be intimate with some people, nor they with us. Perhaps a person who is too afraid of being close will not allow us to be intimate. So, we turn to manipulations to protect ourselves or because we just don't care enough.

The dictionary defines the word "manipulate" as "to work, operate with the hands."* So we could define manipulation as anything that we do. But the further definition includes the words "artful" and "shrewd." And here, I believe, is the source of our confusion. We believe that those who manipulate do so because they want to and we respond, considering their intent, with further manipulations. Frankly, I don't think manipulators play their games because they want to. I believe that we manipulate because we learned how to do it in childhood and because that was what we had to do in order to survive in our particular families. We manipulate because we learned how to behave in that way from our parents, as they learned from their parents. We continue to manipulate because we don't know any other way to behave and because our beliefs about that behavior have not been challenged.

Besides that, change causes stress and intimacy can hurt. Who wants to open oneself up to another person, to say, "Look, this is the real me," and then be rejected or laughed at or put down? Maybe it takes some initial frustration to give impetus to our decision to risk intimacy or the loneliness that goes along with manipulative relationships. Nonetheless, it does take a real decision to stop playing games and risk being hurt in order to establish open, feeling relationships with other people. It takes a decision to come out from behind the mask, and it takes awareness. Without awareness we are stuck in our manipulations and don't know how to stop. With awareness we can drop the manipulation if we want to; or if we still choose to manipulate, at least we know what we're doing!

So what then is manipulation? And how do we stop? I find myself hovering on the brink of a chasm of definitions, yet I keep coming back to one word—control. Manipulation, in my book, is control—of others but also of myself. The opposite of manipulation is response—responding appropriately to others as I feel and as they exist in the here and now. If I want to stop manipulating, I will

*David B. Guralink, Ed.-in-Chief, *Webster's New World Dictionary of the American Language* (New York, Second College Edition, Cleveland, Ohio, William Collins & World Publishing Co., Inc., 1976), p. 862.

stop trying to control others; and I will stop trying to control my feelings about others (although I may want to control my acting out of those feelings). How do I stop controlling? I challenge my belief system, I question my parent messages, and I feel, I feel, I feel!

I want to emphasize that if you catch yourself in a manipulation, you're not automatically wrong. You don't need to be defensive just because you manipulate. Join the crowd. We all do at times. If someone analyzes your manipulation and diagnoses you as sick or crazy or bad for behaving the way you do—and stops there—that person may have a problem. Someone who is truly trying to help you drop your manipulative way of dealing with the world would be allowing you to understand your reasons and your feelings behind your behavior. Anyone who simply criticizes you for feeling as you do or categorizes your behavior is no help to you. So you're depressed or you use your helplessness to get others to take care of you or you take drugs or you're phobic or hysteric or crazy. My question is, *why*? Not what—I take it for granted that we're all manipulators, if at no other time then under stress. But why? And finding the answer to that question, if you're willing to dig into yourself, may take the rest of your life.

I encourage you to start finding your answer, to drop your particular way of controlling others now. Because if you're stuck in your manipulation, not only are you missing the joy of intimate relationships, but you're hurting. The fact is, when you control others by some means, you use the same kind of control on yourself. If you criticize others around you harshly, you're constantly criticizing yourself. If you play helpless you begin to feel helpless and soon you really are. If you control others through hypochondria, you are most likely sick a lot. If you're into the drug scene (pills, booze, tobacco, whatever) or you overeat you can get rid of your anger on those who try to make you quit, but it's your body that's hooked. It's you who suffers the most from your manipulation of others. It's your defense against pain, but it still hurts you.

So, become aware of your manipulation. Do some thinking about how you control your particular world, the people around you, and your own body in the process. Then quit stuffing the knowledge of your manipulations down into the recesses of your mind. Get acquainted with them. Praise your manipulations, sing about them, hold them up to full view. Bring them out in the open so you can examine them. In fact, brag about them. We did this in one of my groups recently. One member said, "I'm the best accuser in the whole world. I accuse so well I can think of accusations nobody else can. I even accuse myself better than anybody!" Another said, "I'm a fantastic withdrawer. When I get angry I shut up and sometimes stay silent for days. Nobody can get to me when I withdraw, and boy, do they feel bad about it." Someone else said, "I talk more than anyone. Whenever I get upset with my family my mouth starts to race. Nobody can get a word in. They don't even try anymore." Another said, "I'm so nice. Even if I hate a person I'm sweet. I smile and smile until my jaws ache. Nobody knows what I'm really thinking. Whenever I'm that nice I get a stomach-ache." As these people did, discover when you use your manipulations, how you control yourself and others, and how your body feels as you do so. After you exaggerate and magnify them, kiss them goodbye and let them go.

I have long been aware that the "Rescue Game" is a part of most manipulations. I have learned to look for it in every conflict and usually find that each partner, often the entire family, is busily engaged in rescuing. In Transactional Analysis, this concept has been diagrammed by Stephen Karpman as the Drama Triangle:

I like to draw the Victim on the bottom to show that victims are usually in the strongest position. Why? Because they indeed have a problem, and it is the Rescuer who is most often defeated. Usually the Victim begins the game with a complaint or description of a problem. The Rescuer responds with a solution. But, not being in the Victim's shoes, the Rescuer really has no idea how the Victim feels. Any problem-solving by the Rescuer is specious and an insult to the Victim's intelligence. By proposing solutions to the Victim's

*The Drawing of the Drama Triangle is from "Fairytales and Script Drama Analysis" by Stephen Karpman, M.D. (*Transactional Analysis Bulletin, Vol. 7, No. 26*, April 1968). Copyright 1968, The International Transactional Analysis Association, Inc. and Stephen Karpman. Reprinted by permission of the ITAA and Stephen Karpman.

problem, the Rescuer is denying the Victim's ability to solve the problem. The Victim, feeling resentful because the Rescuer has not recognized him or her as a cognizant human being, moves into the Persecutor position. The Persecutor then takes it out on the Rescuer, who has by now moved into the Victim position. Rescuing is a great way of getting put down.

I should know. I am a longtime Rescuer and can remember feeling persecuted many times. One of my most painful memories is of the time in graduate school when I tried to help a girl friend. I believed that she was overwhelmed by the pressures of school work and studying for a part in a play. I tried to ease her load by taking over her part for one performance. She said nothing until the final night neared. Then, with other class members standing around, she let me know clearly and vociferously that she did not want my help; she had never wanted my help and she could do her own part in the play. I can still feel the pain of that incident as I write this. I was shocked and hurt and in my head was the classic Rescuer lament, "But I was only trying to help you!"

Inherent in the Rescue Game are two opposites: grandiosity and discounting. A Rescuer who rescues a Victim is acting in a grandiose manner—pompous, self-important, and inspired by a false sense of power. The Victim feels discounted by the Rescuer— ignored, diminished, and insulted. And, in moving into the Persecutor position, the Victim gets his or her original power back. In the above example I felt self-important and protective when I tried to help my girlfriend. She felt resentful because I had discounted her feelings and her ability to help herself. And when she exploded in anger, in the Persecutor position, she proved that she was more powerful than I.

Victims want not to be rescued but to be recognized. They want recognition in order to prove their existence. To illustrate this game, I remember a former class member, Jane B., who was continually rescuing her mother-in-law and feeling put down by the old woman. Their conversation would invariably start with the mother-in-law complaining about some problem, such as "Nobody comes to visit me anymore. I'm so lonely."

Jane would ask, "Why don't you get out more? You have lots of people you could go see." Her mother-in-law would counter with,

"Yes, but I can't. I'm too crippled to walk and my car is broken down."

Jane would suggest, "Why don't you ask someone to come over then? I know they'd be glad to." But her mother-in-law would say, "Yes but I can't. My house is too dirty."

When Jane said, "Well, why don't you get someone in to clean it? You can afford that," the reply would be, "Oh, I couldn't trust someone to do that. They might break something."

This type of conversation went on and on until Jane felt so worn down and defeated she gave up. When we talked about this in class I recognized the moves perfectly. I've played most of them. I suggested that instead of rescuing, Jane simply stroke or recognize her mother-in-law's feelings. We role-played it out and she said she would try it. The next class period Jane was jubilant. She had tried it and it worked. It did not change the mother-in-law particularly but at least Jane felt better. The conversation had begun the usual way, with the mother-in-law saying, "I'm so sick today, my head hurts and my arthritis is acting up and nobody cares."

This time instead of attempting to solve her problems Jane stroked her feelings: "You must feel very lonely over here all by yourself."

The mother-in-law stopped, taken aback. Then she tried a new tack. "Yes, I do. And I can't go anywhere because my car is broken down."

"It must be frustrating for you to have to stay in," said Jane sympathetically.

Her mother-in-law replied, "Yes and I don't know what to do about it."

Jane agreed, "I would feel helpless in that situation too. I don't know a thing about cars."

Jane said that she was strongly tempted to rescue many times but she did not. She simply listened and responded to her mother-in-law's feelings. Eventually the old lady solved her own problem; "I guess I'll have to call up the garage and have them send someone out to fix the car," she sighed, and Jane replied, "That's a very good idea."

Jane gave herself a secret pat on the back. She had learned how to stay out of the Rescue Game.

Jane deserved her pat on the back. It is not easy to identify the Rescue Game, let alone to learn how to avoid it. Rescuers and Victims are trained for their roles and the Game pervades relationships within our society. I was trained to rescue my mother, that is, to take responsibility for her feelings, to take care of her in an emotional sense. I remember feeling resentful when someone would say to me in parting, "Now, take care of your mother." But I tried to do just that by suppressing my feelings.

My little girl is allowed to express her feelings. Once when we both had colds she and I went to the doctor together. As we were leaving the doctor said to her, "Now, take care of your mother!" She made a face as if she had swallowed a lemon.

"That was obviously the wrong thing to say," I told him.

"It didn't sound so great, now that I think about it," he said. He tried again. "Now, you help your mother!" She made the face again.

"That still didn't do it," I said. He quit trying and said, "goodbye." "Honey," I said to her afterwards, "you don't have to take care of me. *I'll* take care of *you* because you're a little kid, and little kids need taking care of." In no way do I want my little girl programmed into being a helpful Rescuer. I'll be satisfied if she learns how to take good care of herself.

Victims, unlike Rescuers, are trained to feel helpless, hopeless, and incompetent. Victims are trained to have people do things for them. If others do not do enough for the Victims, they can always blame others for their failure to take care of them. Perhaps that is one reason the Victim position is so strong. Not only do Victims feel too weak to change their position, they can also evade taking responsibility for themselves while blaming others.

Persecutors are angry and show it. People in the Persecutor position are mean, vengeful, picky, obnoxious, nasty, hateful or even vicious. Persecutors often take advantage of would-be Rescuers, at which point the Rescuer becomes a Victim. I became aware of myself in the Persecutor position when I realized that at times I felt a twinge of meanness. I learned to recognize the feeling but not to act it out. The way out of the Rescue Game is to become aware of your feelings and stop acting on them.

I become very aware of my feelings of pomposity when a Victim complains. I have learned to keep my mouth shut tight when I start to puff up with a feeling of self-importance, thinking I can solve someone else's problem. This does not mean that I always resist the temptation to play the Rescuer successfully. But now when I get put down by a Persecutor, at least I know what happened. It may not make the hurt go away but it helps to know why I'm hurting! When I uncovered my Rescuer role I began to see myself clearly in the Victim and Persecutor positions as well. It was harder to see myself in the latter two, particularly in the Victim position, because the feelings I got into were so much more painful. I didn't like to experience my childhood feelings of fear, loneliness, and hurt. It was much safer to feel either pompous or mean. But I began to realize that if I was in one position, I was in them all. And by getting out of the Rescuer role I was able for the most part to get out of the other two positions as well.

But what does all this have to do with relationships in America today? How do American men and women play the game? And how, if the Victim feels so helpless can he or she be in the strongest position? One of my clients, Susanne O., gave me new insight into these questions recently. She was telling me about her marriage, which was in the process of breaking up. She explained that she had been married for fifteen years and for eight of those years the relationship had been good. She had stayed at home, taking care of her two sons (one from a previous marriage). Then when the younger boy turned seven she tried to get a job. Her husband, Jim, exploded with anger and insisted she stay at home. From that time on the relationship went downhill.

"When I first met Jim I was just divorced and with a new baby on my hands," she said. "He swept me and my baby boy up in his arms and carried us away to a safe haven. I sat back and let him make all the decisions and do everything for us. I'm a hero-maker, I am. I was a real victim—sweet, passive, and dependent. As long as I stayed that way, he was the big hero. He could take care of us and protect us and feel needed. But when I wanted to go out and get a job, even for a half day a week, he felt threatened. His existence as a hero was at stake. I guess from that time on we were done. I couldn't play at being passive anymore; I'm really not that way at all. The more I spoke my mind, the more defensive and angry Jim

became. But I couldn't go back. I'm just not a hero-maker anymore."

Her definition of herself as hero-maker reverberated in my
head as I considered the implications. For Susanne is not the only
hero-maker in America. We are a nation of hero-makers and
psuedoheroes. But what of the real heroes and heroines—were
there none? Of course they existed—in countless numbers—men
who crossed the continent and pioneered the land, who fought the
wars and tamed the wilderness, who were brave and strong and
entirely worthy of being called "heroes." They had real heroines
beside them, women who helped their men fight the battles and
plant the crops, who tended the sick and raised the children, women
well deserving in my opinion of the title "heroines."

But the harsh realities of the pioneer gave way to the cloying
ideals of the romantic. In time women were no longer expected, nor
did they expect, to participate in the carving out of a country. They
were expected to be delicate, fragile, and in terrible need of male
protection. Women in our culture were put on a pedestal and told to
stay there. And stay there they did, with a vengeance. The "wo-
manly" ideal came to be synonymous with passivity, timidity, and
dependence. Any female who dared to assert herself, to compete
intellectually with men, to exert her powers as a human being, was
judged masculine and aggressive. So women became hero-makers.
They learned to stay in the Victim role, to manipulate from a position of helplessness, to use every game in the book—flattery, sickness, petulance, dependence, teasing, inconsistency and guilt—to
manipulate their men.

But did they manipulate their men into being heroes? Real
heroes do not need to keep others dependent on them in order to
prove their masculinity. But there are degrees of heroes, the ingre-
dients of which are the same—strength, bravery, and daring. Who
knows if that bravery is only a facade to cover a palpitating heart
until it is put to the test? And who knows if that strength is only
unwillingness to communicate and the daring merely bravado?
Whether or not the man is a real hero or a pseudohero he is still
expected to perform as a hero in order to protect his helpless mate.
Again I want to stress that I am not pointing my finger or imputing

blame. Neither American men nor American women developed their philosophy and behavior out of malicious intent. Nonetheless, our particular culture and history have trained us to become hero-makers and heroes, victims and rescuers.

The strength of the hero-maker role is clear to me. As a victim the hero-maker can get men to do things for her, to carry her, to take responsibility, to work for her, and to protect her. Why should any bona fide Victim trade her role for one in which she is forced to go out and fend for herself in an uncaring world, and to take full responsibility for her feelings, actions, thoughts, and decisions? It is much easier to allow her hero to do all those tasks, and then blame him if he does what she considers to be the wrong thing. Why compete at all when she can have her hero compete for her?

I remember one session I had with a hero-maker. Agnes J. called me and told me about her deep depression. She said that she did not think the session would do any good but a friend had told her to call me. She explained that her husband had lived out of the state for the past two years. During this time she had believed that as soon as his new business was established, she would sell the house here and join him. Then she got a phone call from him one day during which he asked for a divorce.

"You had no idea he wanted a divorce before this?" I asked.

"None," she said. "Bob and I have always gotten along beautifully."

I felt tired after our session. She would take no responsibility for their breakup. I explained that one person cannot be to blame for all the problems within a relationship, but she would not buy that. She firmly believed that their breaking up was entirely her husband's fault.

During the next session, with her husband present, Agnes seemed confused. She asked him "why" many times. Bob would not give specific explanations. He expressed a great deal of concern for Agnes, but said he just wanted "out." He said that his job had required that he travel away from home for most of their twenty years of marriage and he had grown away from her. She hastened to add that she had raised the children by herself most of the time and had accepted his absences without complaint.

"That's not true," Bob said. "You complained constantly. You wouldn't go out and get a job, you just sat at home and complained. I couldn't do anything right for you either. I tried hard at first."

"I had no idea you thought that," Agnes said. "Why didn't you tell me you were so unhappy?"

"I tried but you wouldn't hear me," he said. "So I gave up. It was easier to stay away from home."

"That's not fair," Agnes said. "Why didn't you yell and scream and shake me before you quit trying?"

"It wouldn't have helped," Bob said. "And besides, I didn't want to hurt you."

I began to see a picture of unexpressed feelings, long standing resentments, and continual rescuing. Bob seemed to be a very nice man. He smiled a lot during our session. He was polite and considerate. He believed strongly that children should not be subjected to divorce. So he had supported his family until the children were grown. As soon as the youngest boy went to college, he informed Agnes that he wanted a divorce. I suspected that he had wanted one for a long time.

"Tell me honestly now," I asked him, "just how long have you been thinking about divorcing Agnes?"

Bob thought for a moment, then without hesitation he said, "Fifteen years."

Agnes almost fell out of her chair. Bob had truly been a hero for all of those lonely married years. He had protected Agnes from fending for herself with young children. He had protected her from his own anger. He had protected her so well that now, at forty-seven, Agnes had no skill or experience in any career. Bob had suffered too, during those years without complaint. He had been unhappy, lonely, and overworked. He had had little fun or joy out of life. But he had a feeling of justification. He had sacrificed his youth for his family. He had little hope of trying again, nor did he particularly want to.

Agnes, on the other hand, was already thinking of finding someone else. She knew the odds were against her; the ratio of single women to eligible men becomes greater the older one gets. Agnes had sat at home for years convincing herself that her children needed all her time and she had no right to a life of her own. She too had sacrificed her youth for her family. She had neither trained for a career nor developed social interests. She too felt the future held little hope. She had done nothing for so long she had little confidence in ever finding a job, let alone a new mate. She was now in the backwater of the job and marriage market, unwanted and out of date.

Martin P. is another very hard worker. Not only does he work hard in his business, he also works hard at life. Even sex is work to him. Martin's religious upbringing had included the message that sex was for procreation. When he married Marian, he complied with his church's teachings until their rapidly growing family numbered six children. Then Marian, a convert to Martin's religion, said "enough." From that day on their sexual relationship declined. When they first came to me, Marian summed it up as "enough has become none at all."

"We never have sex anymore," she complained. "If I suggest it he's too tired, or he has to get up early to go to the office, or he has a headache. Would you believe that? *He* gets a headache. Sometimes I think he's got another woman on the side."

Martin shifted uneasily in his chair. "Oh, that's not true, Marian. When would I have the time? And I wish you weren't always yakking about sex. We have a good relationship, especially when you shut up."

"It's been over six months," Marian started, but Martin silenced her with a wave of his hand.

"Marian thinks that all I have to do is to cater to her impulses," Martin said apologetically to me. "She will not realize that I get tired when I work hard and I have to work hard to support her and our six children. And if you remember," he turned accusingly to Marian, "you wanted all of our children as much as I did so don't blame me like you usually try to do."

"*I* wanted them?—" Marian began.

"Let's get back to sex," I said. Sometimes, in sessions with couples, I feel as if I'm a bulldog, continually pulling both parties back to the issue. "What is your idea of a good sexual relationship, Marian?" I asked.

"Sex should be for fun," she said without hesitation. "It shouldn't be a job to be done, or a duty to be performed. Come to think about it, we don't have fun in anything. We used to have tons of fun before we were married. We'd do things together and go places; we really enjoyed being with each other. I guess the fun started going as soon as we were married, even before we had the children. From then on it was work, work, work. Sex was only the last to go."

"What is your idea, Martin?" I asked.

"Marian thinks we should act like a couple of teenagers forever," Martin said. "She refuses to admit that we are getting older and the juices aren't what they were then. She insists that I give her all my attention. She resents my job but she sure likes the money it brings in."

"What do you think about sex?" I insisted.

"Sex is great, it's here to stay," Martin sidestepped.

"How do you see your sexual relationship with Marian?" I asked.

"I think it's okay," he said finally. "She has nothing else to do with her time than to worry about how I'm treating her. If she had something to do that engrossed her she wouldn't have so much time on her hands to bitch. Frankly, I don't have much time or energy for sex. Before we got married we had all the time in the world for each other. And we did have a lot of fun. That's the purpose of courtship—to have fun together, get to know each other. But marriage is different. After we got married we had to forget all that and settle down, build something. And we have."

"That's right," Marian said. "We have. We've got an expensive waterfront home, property, stocks and bonds, a bank account that'll carry us for a year, and we still don't have any fun!"

"What else is marriage for except to build something?" Martin asked.

"It's to enjoy," Marian answered.

Martin and Marian screamed at each other for a few sessions with me. Marian reported to me that she felt a little better towards Martin because they were clarifying issues that had confused them for years.

"We've always been able to scream at each other," she said. "But I usually don't know what Martin is talking about. I guess he hasn't known what I've meant either. It's been like he's been screaming in Greek and I've been screaming in Latin. We can see each other's lips moving and hear the noise but that's about all it's amounted to. We never have come close to understanding each other."

"Are you understanding each other a little better now?" I asked.

"Yes, I am," she said. "I don't know about him. And the more I understand about him the less I like. I don't know if I'm going to want to stay married to him after all this. But I'm not ready to leave him yet. I know he needs me."

Martin had similar misgivings. "Maybe I shouldn't be married," he said. "I can't give Marian all the time she demands and do my job too. I thought for a long time that she was content, that she had a fulfilling life. But since the children have gotten older and need her less she's become more and more unhappy. We've been married almost thirty years. Maybe that's too long."

Both agreed, however, that they were not yet ready to seriously consider a divorce. They negotiated on several points and came to an agreement of a sort. Martin agreed to give Marian more attention when he was home and set up at least one evening a week that was all hers. Marian agreed to find some type of work that she enjoyed to help fill some of the time vacated by her maturing children. They stopped coming to therapy sessions, both expressing the belief that they did not need to work on personal problems, just their decaying relationship.

Marian called me a few months later. She and Martin were still together, still unhappy, still screaming at each other, and still toying with the thought of divorce. Although each professed to understand the other much better after our sessions together, each refused to accept the other's philosophy. Marian refused to become the worker Martin was, nor would Martin take time and energy away from his job to go off and play with Marian. Neither had fulfilled the terms of their previous agreement. Marian had looked for a job cursorily; when she had not found one immediately she had given up trying. Martin had consistently found other obligations more pressing than his weekly evening with Marian. Each wanted the other to change but refused to initiate any major change in his or her lifestyle.

Nor did either really understand that they continually rescued each other. Marian would not see herself as a hero-maker, although she had responded to Martin's needs, at least her fantasy of his needs, for almost thirty years. If she was angry at Martin for not giving her attention, she was partially to blame. When he came home tired she catered to his fatigue. If she wanted attention from him in any form she would not convey her desires to him openly. Her demands on him were usually expressed long after the situation had passed in the form of recriminations. Marian nagged. Her nagging put Martin in a double bind. She wanted Martin to continue to earn his above-average income yet she nagged about the amount of time he spent away from home. She made no secret of her love of luxury. As much as Marian resented his lack of attention, she loved the money his workaholic habits brought in. She was not willing to share his work load by going into any kind of serious career herself.

Martin was a hero in that he worked hard to build an estate for his family. He rescued Marian by hiding his problems from her. When Marian begged him to tell her about his business problems he would not, believing that he should shoulder his own burdens. He could not understand why Marian resented his secrecy when, as he put it, he was doing it for her own good! He concluded that Marian simply did not appreciate how hard he worked for her and the children. He called his family "ungrateful" and thanked heaven that he had the business to turn to for his feelings of worth and appreciation.

Martin and Marian are still together. Their relationship is by no means secure, because each of them is still considering divorce. They may only stay together until their last child leaves home. On the other hand, they might stay together for many more years, perhaps for their lifetimes. Where else could they find such beautiful cop-outs? Neither has to accept responsibility for his or her bad feelings while they have each other. They do have a type of communication. They can verbalize their anger by screaming at each other, which is perhaps better than the total silence of some couples. A marriage need not be pleasant and healthy for the individuals concerned to stay together. All it takes is the decision to do so. Marian and Martin have decided, at least for the present, to stay married. They have what some have termed an "acrimonious" relationship.

Mike T. was another workaholic. He was one of the strongest men I have ever known, not in physical strength but in his ability to control his feelings. Mike came in to see me because his wife, Barbara, insisted that they see someone. They were thinking of getting a divorce and both felt ambivalent about it. Mike said that they might as well, but he did not want to be the one to initiate divorce proceedings. Barbara said she did not want to break up their home but she did not know what else to do. Mike had moved into his own apartment across town and refused to move back in with her and their three children. Barbara felt upset, not knowing when or if he would ever come back.

Barbara admitted to me that she had had an affair. She said that she had been desperate for human touch. She said that she knew it had been unfair for her to seek love outside her marriage, but she was angry at Mike and tired of trying to comunicate with him. She also said she wanted to save her marriage if somehow she and Mike could learn to talk openly to each other. She said too that she was willing to work on her own problems through therapy.

Mike was not willing to work on his feelings, though he came to individual sessions and talked about himself readily.

"I'm happy where I am," he told me. "I did go to a psychiatrist when Barbara first started stepping out on me. I thought I might be driving her to it in some way. But he told me there was nothing the matter with me. 'Take more vacations,' he said, 'and you'll do fine.' So why should I go into all my hangups in therapy? I'd rather use the money to go to Europe. Besides, she's the one who needs it. I happen to like my life the way it is!"

Somehow, I did not feel convinced. "How come the psychiatrist told you to take more vacations?" I asked him.

"I suppose it's the standard prescription for all his patients," Mike said. "Oh, it's true that I work hard, some have said too hard. But I like my work. I was raised to believe in the Protestant work ethic. I wouldn't know what to do with myself without my work. I admit I put in too many sixteen-hour days, but I enjoy it, so what the hell! I believe in living the way I like to live and not worrying about tomorrow. I like to eat; I'm a gourmet cook, you know. And I enjoy tipping a few now and then."

"Have you ever had any physical problems, anything that could be connected with stress?" I asked.

"Not really," Mike said. "I've learned to pace myself at work pretty well. Oh, I did have a massive coronary five years ago," he said casually. "I was forty-two. The doctors told me then to stop working so hard and relax more. I did for awhile. But I got bored just lying around so I gradually found myself working at my old pace. It doesn't seem to be hurting me. So what if I don't live as long as a guy who sits around doing nothing? I'm living for today, not for ten years from now. I like where I am."

Mike sat back in his chair and reached for another cigarette. He smoked incessantly. As he lit his cigarette, shifting his overweight frame to reach for the ashtray, he grinned at me. It seemed to me to be a rebellious, little boy, try-to-stop-me-if-you-can kind of grin. I saw it many times during the few sessions we had together.

Once I blurted out, "Mike, I like you. I'm so sad that you're going to die!"

"What the hell are you talking about?" he said, his grin fading. "I'm not going to die for a long time."

"Oh, yes, you are," I said. "If you keep smoking and eating and drinking and working as much as you do now, you're surely going to die very young and I'll be very sad."

"Let me worry about that," he said, and he changed the subject.

One day I asked Mike what he had felt when he first learned of Barbara's affair.

"I don't like to think about it," he said. "It still hurts."

"You love her very much, don't you?" I said.

"I did," he replied. "I don't know what I feel now."

"If you've had so much love for her, why are you considering a divorce?" I asked. "How about working with her for a better relationship?"

"She's the one who had the affair. I didn't," he said. "It's her problem, not mine. Besides, I agreed that I would go see someone, and I am. I'm seeing you, right?"

"Yes, you're seeing me, and I'm not sure why," I said. "You're not willing to work on your feelings in any way. You do a lot of talking about yourself, about your experiences, your job, and your desires, but you refuse to talk about your childhood, other than to say you were always happy. You refuse to feel anything, especially your anger towards Barbara."

"It hurts too much," he said. "She hurt me once and I don't want to hurt like that again. And I'm not angry at her. I should feel sorry for her, I suppose. But it's over, so why worry about it. I just don't want to get the divorce. Let her get it, I don't care." He paused and thought for a moment. "I guess the truth is that I have an enormous ego. I can't take that kind of blow to my ego again. I'd rather not love at all. Besides, I have a family who loves me—my mother is still living, my sisters and brothers. I've moved near to them and they appreciate me as Barbara never did. I don't need her kind of love as long as I've got them."

Something about the words "enormous ego" bothered me, but I did not know what it was. I have heard men talk of their enormous egos before and had accepted the term. Now, suddenly, those words made no sense to me. I didn't know what Mike meant by them. That night, I awoke in the middle of the night with the words still running through my head. Man's enormous ego. What ever happened to woman's enormous ego? Why don't women ever talk about their enormous egos; haven't they got them too? Then it all fell into place. Of course! That was it! Mike had no more of an enormous ego than any woman did. Certainly no more than Barbara did although she expressed hers differently, as a need for human touch. And both feelings stemmed from similar sources. Mike simply had an enormous need—just as Barbara had an enormous need—not for other men, not for other women, but for mother and father. One of the youngest of eight children, Mike had an enormous need for attention and love from his parents, especially his mother. When he felt rejected by Barbara, it was not only her rejection of him that hurt but all the times in his childhood that he had felt abandoned or neglected by his mother. So it was natural for him to seek the love he wanted, not with his wife, but with his own mother. It was natural for him to go home to mother—to the family of his childhood—to get the love he needed.

It was also natural for him to continue being a hard worker, despite his doctor's warnings. The work ethic that he professed to believe in was actually a rational explanation for an inner feeling—the need for his father's approval. He had told me that his father had been a hard worker and a disciplinarian and that he had died at the young age of fifty-seven. I suspected that Mike was programming himself to die before his father. If Mike allowed himself to slack off from his work and relax, he would not feel the approval he needed. It was therefore only natural for him to tackle his work with even more determination, whether or not his ailing heart cried out for rest.

Approval and need, keeping himself in tight control, being strong—finally I understood what Mike was all about. I understood what was behind his rebellious grin. I understood that it was a brave grin, a strong grin, a "don't try to make me feel" grin. For he would not feel. I remembered Mike reminding himself one time when the subject we were on touched him too deeply, "Don't feel that, don't feel that."

Although my understanding of Mike increased, I still could not motivate him to express his feelings or to work on his feelings in therapy. He would not accept my permission that it was okay to feel. He quit seeing me shortly thereafter. Nor could Barbara convince him to move back in with her.

Barbara continued to work on her own problems through individual therapy, as she had been doing all along, for a few more sessions. Then she too quit. She told me that although she was gaining increased understanding of herself and was generally feeling better, her marital situation had not changed at all. She called me several months later to say that Mike still refused to come back or to express any of his feelings towards her. She felt that he simply did not care anymore. She said that she had started divorce proceedings.

I wished I could have conveyed to Mike my awareness of his needs, but I had not been able to do so, no matter how I phrased it. My telling him that he was going to die meant absolutely nothing to him. Mike would have had to feel his own terror at being rejected or disapproved of by his parents and he was not willing to feel at all. He would have had to admit his carefully guarded anger at Barbara and release it. Since he was unwilling to reexperience his own childhood needs or his present day feelings, nothing I said to him made any difference in his position.

Nor did anything Barbara said to him make any difference. She had raged at him, she had stormed, she had pouted. Nothing she did would elicit any straight response from him. I suppose he believed, as so many of us do, that he would hurt her feelings if he expressed his anger. He didn't say that to me; all he would ever say was that he was not angry. Yet who can be angrier than a person who simply leaves, and then refuses to talk about it? Mike was rescuing Barbara by remaining silent, and he continued to rescue by allowing her to get the divorce rather than working on their relationship. I imagine he hurt inside a great deal because of his silence and will continue to hurt. But he will also continue to be brave and internalize his pain until one day his ailing heart can take it no longer. Then Mike will join the ranks of those unsung heroes, strong and silent, who yearly add to this country's statistics on heart disease.

Mike was similar to Martin in that he was a hard worker who held his feelings in rather than expressing them readily. He was even stronger than Martin, however, since he expressed none of his feelings of anger. Whereas Martin would at least scream out his anger at Marian to release some of his internal pressure, Mike would not even admit that he was angry at Barbara. He turned all of his anger back onto himself, and it affected him where he was most vulnerable, in his heart.

Martin and Marian are still miserable in their angry, volatile relationship, but they are together. They have decided, at least for the present, to remain in their state of marital war. Mike and Barbara did not make that decision. They got divorced. Actually the divorce decree was only the outward expression of the state of their marriage for years past; whereas Martin and Marian had a bitter relationship, Mike and Barbara had no relationship at all.

Each of the partners in these four marriages was firmly caught in the Rescue Game. Most still are. Barbara T. may have changed enough through therapy to stay out of the Victim role if she remarries. I am not sure if she has changed that much, because she is still blaming Mike totally for their breakup. Barbara, however, believes that because she was willing to work on herself through therapy she has changed. She may be right; only time will tell. I do know that Susanne O., who was able to see herself as a hero-maker, has gotten out of the Rescue Game. By becoming aware of herself in the Victim role, Susanne admitted her own complicity and took responsibility for her part of the marital conflict. She also understood how she had changed from Victim into protective mama. She had rescued Jim too. During their years together Jim had tried very hard to be a success. His way of "making it" was to sell everything and start afresh. On three different occasions he had sold their house and taken his family to another part of the country—once to the

Florida keys to hunt for treasure. That time he ended up digging ditches instead of treasure. The other two expeditions seemed just as futile to Susanne, yet she had said nothing. She believed that a wife should follow her husband wherever he leads. And she did, resenting him bitterly every time she went along with him. Finally she decided she had had enough and refused to move again. She began to get out of the hero-maker role by speaking up. She remained a Victim, however, by continuing to cater to Jim while refusing to change her life. She still hesitated to hurt Jim by telling him exactly what she felt. She did not take the job she wanted because he preferred that she stay home.

Jim did not like even this small change in Susanne's behavior. Instead of talking to her about his feelings he became closed off and defensive. His drinking problem got worse. On a few occasions, while drunk, he beat her. The last time he pushed her against the wall and split her head open. After that Susanne told him that she would leave if he ever beat her again. He stopped drinking and never hit her again, but his anger continued to grow. He expressed it in criticism, sarcasm, and subtle put-downs. When she would confront him he would evade her by saying, "Can't you take a joke?" "You're too sensitive," or "You're imagining things," or not answering at all. Their marriage lasted seven more years. Then Jim refused to have sex with Susanne. He told her he did not love her anymore. Although he refused to admit it, Susanne knew he had found another woman. He blamed Susanne for their breakup. Susanne blamed herself.

One of the biggest problems I have found in couples therapy is the difficulty I encounter trying to convince both partners that each is responsible for his or her own bad feelings. It is too easy for each to blame the other. Susanne accepted responsibility for her feelings, and was able to work on her own growth and continue to change. But Jim, by not accepting responsibility for his feelings, believed that because Susanne was changing she was to blame for all their problems. This left Susanne with two options—either to go back to being a hero-maker or to get out. Actually, Jim presented a third option. He got out. Susanne knew she did not want to be a hero-maker anymore. But because Jim left her, she felt many childhood feelings of abandonment. Had she made the decision to leave, the pain may not have been so great. When Suzanne and I worked on finding the source of her pain, she was able to trace her feelings of loss to her childhood and her relationship with her alcoholic father. She had not actually been abandoned, but because her father had not "been there" for her, even when he was present, she felt a sense of loss.

For several months after Jim left Susanne fought off the temptation to kill herself. During this period of depression she was retroflecting her anger onto herself. Eventually she discovered that her anger could more appropriately be directed towards Jim. She worked on verbalizing her feelings during several therapy sessions. Her depression lifted as she got in touch with and released her rage. She no longer directed self-destructive thoughts towards herself. She was able to realize the depth of her anger toward Jim. Today Susanne continues to change. She understands that she was not entirely to blame for their breakup, nor was Jim. Because she is now able to be open and honest in her expression of feeling, she will undoubtedly meet someone in the future with whom she can interact in an open and loving relationship.

I doubt that she will look for someone to rescue again, judging from some feedback I got recently from a friend of hers. "Susanne has changed so much since she came to you," her friend told me. "She doesn't hesitate to come right out with where she's at. She used to be so—sympathetic. Now sometimes she's positively uncomfortable to be around."

"You mean she doesn't listen to you complain the way she used to?" I asked.

"Heavens, no," her friend said. "She's not nice at all. She told me it was my problem if I was unhappy in my marriage and gave me your phone number. She told me if I really wanted to do something about my problems to set up a session with you. But, you know, I like her better this way. She's the only absolutely straight person I know."

Susanne is no longer a victim and she has quit being a hero-maker. Jim, on the other hand, has already found a substitute hero-maker, whom he can rescue and be rescued by in return. Like so many other men who have been trained since childhood not to feel, he found it absolutely impossible to open himself up to Susanne and reveal his true feelings. He will find it just as impossible with his new mate. How can he be intimate with anyone when he himself does not know what he feels? If he *did* admit his rage towards Susanne rather than blame her for causing it, he would be forced to admit that his extreme anger had little to do with his wife. He would see that his rage was originally directed towards his own parents, most probably his mother, and that he had not been allowed to express it in childhood. He has not admitted his anger, however, and may not even remember feeling it. Like many other people he may have totally blocked his childhood feelings of anger. Like Mike T., he may insist that his parents always treated him with love. So he remains stuck in his manipulative behavior, unwilling to risk intimacy, choosing instead a controlled relationship of a hero to his hero-maker.

Agnes and Bob remain stuck in the Rescue Game even though they have divorced. Each continues to blame the other for their breakup. Neither has taken responsibility for his or her bad feelings, nor are they likely to do so in the future. Each is firmly convinced he (and she) is right. If they remarry I am sure they will both continue the game with their new partners. Agnes will remain the hapless victim and hero-maker, feeling dependent, confused, and helpless. Bob will continue to be the strong, silent hero who feels criticized and used.

Agnes had been confused about Bob's "nice" demeanor, particularly since, as a victim, she never gave herself permission to think. If she had, she would have realized that Bob was not really so nice after all. For in being nice, Bob was only being distant. Never had he said an angry word to her. Certainly he had never struck her, as Jim had Susanne. Bob had always been polite, considerate, and concerned about her. He had protected her and supported her dependence. He had never responded to her "whys" with any show of feelings. He was too nice for that.

Actually Bob's niceness was his manipulation. He practiced being nice as a defense against intimacy. He had been trained since childhood to hold in his feelings, not by expressionless parents, as some have been, but by parents who expressed violent feelings. They had screamed at each other, thrown things at each other, and beat each other. Bob had learned from them that feelings were terrifying. He did not want to be like them, therefore he decided when he was very young not to feel. He believed that to express feelings meant to express violence. When Agnes would get upset with him and demand some expression of feeling, his first impulse was to calm her down. If he could not do that he walked out and calmed himself down.

I assumed that Bob was an angry man under all his niceness. I know that any two people in a relationship get angry at each other occasionally. If they do not express it, they retain it. I knew that since Bob had not expressed his anger toward Agnes he had held it in for all those years. But Bob denied this. He insisted he was not angry with Agnes, only sorry for her. He was totally unwilling to get in touch with his anger. I have known others like Bob who, being terrified of feelings when they were small, fear that their anger can kill. So, rather than risk killing their parents or their mates, they hold their rage in and deny its existence. If Bob was unwilling to feel, I could not force him into awareness. Nor could anyone. No one can *force* another person to feel or grow.

So Bob will go on being nice and burying his anger. He may marry again, like Jim, choosing another hero-maker. But unlike Jim, Bob will distance himself from his new mate by being nice and considerate to the point of self-denial. He will not express his negative feelings for his new mate because he is afraid of them. He will not be able to express his tender feelings for long because his resentments will soon get in the way. Instead of expressing any feeling then, he will build a barrier of politeness that will substitute for love.

Most men today believe they should be strong, forceful, and brave. If there is a men's liberation movement it so far has had little impetus. Men are encouraged by our changing social norms far less than women to change their roles. But there are many men who have dropped the hero role. Will A. did it when he stopped alternating between acting strong for his wife and being the rebellious little boy. Barry W. did it when he stopped driving himself to be a success for his family. Marv S. did it when he stopped trying to perform well sexually. I will grant that it is easier for a man to stop being a hero when the woman with whom he is involved stops being the hero-maker. Games are much easier to break out of when both parties involved stop manipulating at the same time. But when one person stops manipulating the effect spreads to the other family members, like ripples in a pond spreading out from one small stone. These effects are not always good for the relationship, as was the case with Susanne and Jim. Usually, in fact, some agitation results because change is stressful. But if the relationship is basically sound it will survive the shakeup. If it is unhealthy the most positive step the individuals could take would be away from each other.

So how do you stop being a hero or a hero-maker? Perhaps the most important element to keep in your head is the "stroke." A stroke, in Transactional Analysis, is a unit of social recognition. I think of strokes as both positive and negative. A positive unconditional stroke ("I love you," "I like you for who you are") is the kind of stroke we all want but get too rarely. We more often get positive conditional strokes ("I like the way you wear your hair"). We are a performance-oriented society, so we get most of our negative strokes in the conditional form too ("I don't like your housekeeping," "I don't like the way you talk," "I don't like your reports"). Even unconditional negative strokes are okay to use ("I don't like you," "I hate you").

A good way to give a negative stroke is to precede it with a positive one. If you are angry with someone close to you, for example, you might say, "I love you very much *and* I am very angry with you right now." Use "and," not "but." "But" negates any prior stroke. If you are speaking to a co-worker or an acquaintance you might say, "I respect you and your ideas *and* I feel irritated by what you just said."

We all want attention. In essence, a stroke is attention—it is recognition of our existence. When someone gives you a stroke, that person is saying, "Hello, you exist to me." If you do not get any strokes you are discounted. You may begin to feel that you are invisible and that you really do not exist. All of us at all ages need strokes. Babies need strokes in the form of physical touch and caressing. If babies do not get enough strokes they may wither away and die. Children need strokes in the form of physical touch and verbal communication. A child who is not getting positive strokes may turn into a delinquent in order to get negative strokes, because any kind of stroke is better than none at all. Negative recognition is still recognition of a sort and helps validate one's existence. Even spankings and beatings are better than being ignored. Some people may even resort to self-mutilization in order to get attention.

Certainly there is such a thing as "discounting the bad behavior," that is, ignoring some irritating habit and giving the child some positive reinforcement instead. For example, rather than continually criticize the child for biting his nails, try ignoring the habit for a change; after he stops, give him a hug for just being.

But other kinds of discounting can be detrimental to the child's sense of self. I heard of one family that made a practice of ignoring each other. The teenage son got very angry one day and hit the wall with his fist, making a large hole in it. Nobody, not his father, mother, brothers or sisters, said a word about it. I can imagine that boy's someday resorting to more violent behavior in order to feel visible to others.

I remember saying one day to a class, "It's okay for anyone to express feelings, even for a little child to say to his parents 'I hate you!' " One man got very upset with me.

"You're wrong," he said loudly. "Children should respect their parents."

"What do your kids do with their feelings?" I asked him. "If your son got angry with you or your wife, how could he express it?"

"I don't care what he does outside the home, but in the home our kids respect their parents," he replied.

Respect, in this case, sounded to my ears very much like discounting.

Grownups need strokes too. A person may become chronically depressed if he or she is not getting enough strokes. In our country, believing as we do in the myth of marital happiness, we think that we should get all our strokes from our marital partners. Men are usually not as severely oppressed by this belief because they hold jobs outside the home more commonly than women. But a woman in the home without access to the community through a career may suffer a stroke deficit. Mothers in particular, who are tied down by young children and financial limitations, may have problems getting enough strokes. The home-bound mother is often unable to get enough strokes from her children, for their demands outweigh their ability to give to others. So she will look to her husband, expecting that he should give her more strokes. The more she demands, the less he will be likely to give. And the less he gives, the more she will demand. She will become caught in a circle of emptiness, not knowing how to break out, truly stroke-starved.

No one person is capable, no matter how loving he or she may be, of filling another person's stroke bank. Each one must fill his or her own by getting enough strokes for personal satisfaction. I usually recommend to clients that they develop a "Stroke List" of ways they might get strokes. You can do this for yourself. Put on your list the names of people who will give you strokes, those with whom it is okay to ask for what you need. Then add things to do that you have enjoyed in the past, things you have never done that sound like fun, and any specific way you know of to feel good. My Stroke List might include taking a walk on the beach, asking my husband for a hug, reading a novel, taking a bubble bath, going out to lunch in a fancy restaurant, calling a special friend, and signing up for a painting class. Put at least a dozen ways to get strokes on your list. Then when you need refueling, instead of trying to prod your listless brain to work, you can just pick an item from your Stroke List and go.

The person who is not getting strokes and does not know how to ask for them, will manipulate. Therefore, the quickest way to cut through the manipulation is to give the other person a positive stroke. Have you ever, for example, sat down to read your paper after a long, tough day and had your little kid come up to you with, "I wanna tell you what happened at school today." If you responded with, "Not now, I'm reading," you were in for it, right? What little kid takes no for an answer? More than likely that was the start of his acting out—screaming, bouncing up and down, rattling his drum set—until you either yelled at him to be quiet or spanked him. A negative stroke is better than none at all. If you had listened to him in the first place and given him a hug or a positive verbal stroke (e.g., "Hey, you did all right today."), you would have both been spared the unceasing demand for a negative stroke.

A positive stroke doesn't have to be a compliment. If someone is really manipulating you may not be able to sincerely give that person a positive stroke. And certainly, if you flatter, he or she will pick up your insincerity. What you can do is to recognize that person's feelings. Practice listening for feelings rather than words. Other people may talk about what they are thinking and what they are doing. They may not know what they are feeling. So listen around and between the words, then check out what you think you're hearing—"You sound like you're feeling defeated," or whatever. Very often the person will respond, "Why, yes, that's what

I'm feeling. I hadn't thought about that before." And you might share similar feelings you have experienced: "I've felt the same way before in a position like yours." Recognition of feelings may not be the same kind of positive stroke as an "I like you" is; nonetheless you will both *feel* stroked if you have the chance to openly share your feelings.

A part of our cultural problem with relationships is that men are supposed to be logical in their approach to life while women are seen as emotional creatures. Men have been trained to think through problems rather than respond with their feelings. When confronted with a problem men will generally try to find an intellectual solution. While this approach may solve business problems, it does nothing for a relationship. A woman, for example, will voice a problem concerning her feelings, such as "I'm bored." The man will problem-solve, "Why don't you find something to do?" This is a rescue. They are immediately off and running in a game with the woman trying to prove she has a reason for feeling the way she does and the man attempting heroically to provide her with a solution. The Rescuer fails to realize that no one can make anyone else feel any different if she refuses to change. He cannot make her happy. He cannot give her answers. He probably does not even know the question!

Each one of us knows, deep inside ourselves, the answer to our problems. If the woman's problem concerns her feelings, the approach most likely to help is to stroke, or recognize her feelings. For example the man might say, "You seem bored!" By validating her feelings in this way he allows the woman to find her own solution for feeling better. He might encourage her to solve her own problem by saying, "What would feel good to you?" He will avoid the popular game of "Why don't you. . . . Yes but. . . ." When he validates her feelings he gives her the greatest stroke of all—his attention. He might follow up the stroke with an offer of help, "Is there anything you want me to do?" He could also share his feelings, "I've been bored too lately. Let's find something to do to get some fun into our lives."

I don't mean to imply here that this situation never happens the other way around. Certainly women rescue; they have been trained to take care of the feelings of everybody around them too. Within the Rescue Game the hero-maker can change from dependent victim to protective mama to vengeful bitch and back again within a few moment's time, while the pseudo-hero can change from protective daddy to nasty little kid to petulant sufferer just as quickly. I'm generalizing when I say, "Men are supposed to be logical." Of course I know, and you know, that men are not intrinsically more logical than women, but they are *supposed* to be—just as women are not the sole keepers of emotions, but they are *supposed* to be. Therefore, though each has, in my mind, equal potential to think and to feel, they do not have equal societal permission. And since denial of permission amounts to a should, many men and women have learned to control their expression of emotions or of thoughts in culturally approved ways. So when I say that men will generally try to find an intellectual solution to a problem, I mean that it has been my experience that more men think through problems while, generally, more women feel their way through.

Women have been culturally trained, in their hero-maker roles, to allow their heroes to take the first step. Even if women know exactly what they want they have generally been taught to hint rather than tell men openly. So the woman who voices a feeling may have a fairly good idea of how to solve her problem. But instead of acting on her feeling, she may wait for the man to offer a solution. Then she can tell him how brilliant he is for having thought of something she knew all the time. If she is manipulating in this way, she is probably belittling him in her own mind for not having thought of the solution sooner. And if he sustains her dependency by continuing to solve all her problems, he will probably find his steps slowing as the weight of his burden increases.

Another problem confronting heroes and hero-makers is that they have been taught to be absolutely loyal to the other. Women particularly have been taught that if they have an opinion that differs from their spouse's they should keep it to themselves. I remember one woman in a class of mine who had been married for twenty-five years to a sarcastic, abusive, authoritative man. She despised his methods of disciplining their three girls. She thought he was far too harsh in his punishments, but she did not speak out and the girls thought she approved of her husband's treatment. All three were turning against their mother. She agonized over their angry rebellion, yet she had never shared her opinions and feelings about her husband with them.

She believed very strongly that she had been right to remain loyal to her husband. She would not listen to me when I pleaded with her to share her feelings with her girls. She had made the decision years before to sacrifice her children on the altar of heroism and she was determined to stick to that. Of course, she was not doing it entirely out of loyalty to her husband. A hero-maker remains a victim because she is afraid. She fears that her husband might abandon her, beat her, or lose his love for her if she asserts her real feelings.

Being loyal to one's spouse is not reserved entirely for women. Men are taught to be loyal as well. One man told me that his mother used to beat him with a strap when he was a boy, before he got big enough to outrun her. His father would sit by and do nothing. One day the boy asked his father why, even knowing the punishment was not deserved, he wouldn't do anything. His father told him, "Why, she's your mother, son. I can't cross her. If I did she'd turn against me. Besides, she and I have got to stick together or you kids would walk all over us." Then the explanation seemed to make sense. Today, this man realizes that the words don't make a bit of sense.

It is apparent to me that the major feeling behind both the hero and the hero-maker role is fear, not only the present fear that the spouse might leave but the childhood fear of being abandoned by one's parents. When a person is tempted to be disloyal, both present and archaic fears surface. One group member, working on her feelings for her parents expressed similar fears: "I was afraid to be disloyal to my parents when I was little because I thought they'd kick me out. Even today I'm afraid to say the wrong thing for fear they'll never speak to me again. I feel guilty even talking about them or my husband in group." This woman found in therapy that her particular manipulation was to eat. She had been programmed throughout childhood to see food as a reward. "Have a cookie, dear," her mother would say. "It'll make you feel better," or, "If you're a really good girl I'll buy you an ice cream cone." Whenever she got angry at her parents or, after she married, at her husband, she would stuff down the anger with food. Instead of expressing her feelings, thereby being "disloyal," she would try to make herself feel better by gorging. The fatter she became the more she was able to turn her anger onto herself, thus disguising her anger against her parents and her husband even more. And the more weight she put on the more loyalty she professed—until she started group!

Loyalty is marvelous and most appropriate when loved ones need actual support and sustenance. But being loyal to someone doesn't mean you have to always agree with that person. Disagreeing or being angry with a loved one, is not disloyalty. It's normal, and it's normal to want to get rid of that painful feeling. So go ahead and tell your mate about your feelings. And if your spouse won't let you be open about your feelings, talk to your friends. You're not being disloyal by expressing your feelings; you're showing good sense and taking care of yourself.

When I hear people say they do not want to be disloyal to their mates or family members, I hear them really saying they are afraid to show their anger. It's risky to express anger, even riskier when you don't have permission to do so. We all need to decide for ourselves whether or not to take that risk. If you decide to risk, and if you agree with me that you will have a more positive relationship by verbalizing your feelings, then give each member of your family permission to express his or her feelings directly. Allow your partner to have divergent opinions and feelings. And express your anger to each other in front of the children, although certainly not all the time. A child who never hears parents verbalizing angry feelings toward each other does not gain permission to express anger to his or her future spouse. So give your children that permission by being straight with each other, sometimes within their hearing. No hitting, no accusations, just direct gut-level expressions of feelings. Quit being so "loyal" and keeping a stiff upper lip. You may find that you drop much of your manipulating.

If you find yourself beset by old fears and continually falling back into old manipulations, don't be discouraged. Remember that it took you years to learn your manipulations. It may take you years to *un*learn them—not as many as it took you to learn them in the first place, but years at any rate. When you drop your games you will need to learn new ways of relating to people. You will need time to learn new attitudes and behavior patterns. You will have your whole lifetime. What else have you got to do with your life than grow? Through growing, maturing, opening yourself, you can once again contact your feelings and begin to express them.

7

Feelings

*We can learn to
relate to each other intimately
after we stop playing games.*

Civilization discourages feelings. The pace of life in our culture, the stress of making a living, and the tension of coping in contemporary America all contribute to our turning off our feeling selves. Stress and tension are the great enemies of feeling. So are the messages that we receive continually from parents, teachers, and employers: "Work hard," "Be perfect," "Please your parents," "Hurry up," and "Be strong." These messages are vital to the maintenance of our "civilized" culture. Few of us would show up for a job, get to a class on time, or adapt to our society in any way if we did not obey these commands to some extent. But when the messages are followed explicitly in our personal as well as our public and professional lives they encourage us to turn off our feeling selves.

The message "Be Strong" in particular tells us to think rather than feel. Some of the versions you may have heard may be "Don't cry," "Be brave," "Crybaby!" "Use your head," and "Don't be silly." Our parents have given us these similar messages to help us survive, or so they thought. But to be really strong, to be in complete control of your feelings, means to feel nothing. And that feeling-less state is actually one in which you retain your feelings intact.

Strength, from this point of view, is actually deadness caused by unwillingness to contact your own feelings. I interpret "pride" in much the same way. When people tell me they are too proud to ask for certain things or say certain things I hear them saying they are unwilling to take the risk of feeling. So they cop out by being proud or strong. If they were not so proud they would allow themselves to be less controlled, in touch, responding to the here and now with their feeling selves.

Babies are born feeling people. They are taught to repress and control their feelings as they grow up. They are taught how to act and what they are permitted to feel, depending on their sex, race, economic status, location, and parental values. Boys are taught that they should use their heads, act aggressively, and hide their tears. Girls are taught that they should use their tears, act sweetly, and hide their anger. Some boys and girls are taught to be independent and support themselves; others are trained to rely on society for their needs. Some are taught that they are the chosen few; others are taught that they are the outcasts of society. Whatever the specific messages, whatever the particular bias, the result is that most children learn to turn off their feelings and adapt in some way to their parents' messages.

I have said earlier that women have more permission to feel than do men. Generally, I do find it easier to help a woman get in touch with her feelings. In therapy sessions, more men will talk about their feelings from an intellectual point of view rather than feel them. I believe the reason for this is that most men received so much cultural programming about being strong that they have been taught to be, on the average, far more controlled. I have become aware, however, that women have as many prohibitions as men about expressing certain feelings, for example, elation, joy, exultation, aggressiveness, and anger. Our culture gives women permission to feel *bad*. They are allowed to feel blue, tired, sad, lonely, and bored. They are allowed to cry a lot. Women are also allowed to be depressed. Men are allowed to feel angry, excited, competitive, and exultant. Men may brag about their accomplishments (unlike women), but they are not supposed to feel sad or lonely. Men are not supposed to dwell on feelings; they are supposed to think about things. Put concisely, in our culture women are encouraged to complain, men to explain.

My personal growth classes for women have been popular and well attended while my growth courses for men and women together often fail. I believe the reason for this is that women, who are supposed to have bad feelings, are seeking relief and personal change. Women seem more willing to share their problems with someone else, someone who may tell them how to feel better. Many women are more than willing to listen, but remain helpless and hurting. They have such permission to feel bad that they will not even try to change that position. Men, having been taught to be strong, are more likely to try to solve their emotional problems themselves. Some do it out of sheer will. But it's tough to will away a relationship problem. If they have a hint that all is not well with their relationship, they may reject it immediately. Men, who are not supposed to feel weak or helpless, have usually convinced themselves that nothing needs to be changed. Nor do they usually want to look too closely. If they looked, they might see feelings inside themselves they're not supposed to have. My own husband put this concisely to me awhile ago when we were talking about some problems we were having. "I never look inside myself," he said, "except when you make it necessary." I went into hysterics.

It is tough for a man to retain his culturally approved image as a pillar of strength if he is crying from gut-level fear and loneliness. I remember a man who experienced childhood feelings of loneliness during one class. Before that time he had had no memories of being lonely as a child. When he contacted his feelings he realized that he had been lonely many times as a child and still was as a grown man. His wife told me later that she had asked him about some of these experiences immediately after the class. "Lonely?" he said. "I was never lonely when I was a kid." He had denied his feelings immediately after he had felt them.

This man, like many others I know, had built a shell of intellectualism and efficiency around his inner vulnerability. A business executive in a large corporation, he had a keenly analytical mind and a gift for sarcastic innuendoes. He was held in awe by his colleagues, most of whom feared him. His wife and two children, however, had a great deal of resentment toward him because he would not share his feelings with them. He distanced himself from them by his continual criticism, delivered in a reasonable and compassionless manner. He could not allow himself to share his inner feelings of loneliness with them for fear that his entire protective structure might crumble. He had to deny his vulnerability in order to keep intact his defense of a penetrating mind.

I know of some men who deny their feelings to the extreme of not going to the doctor when they have some physical ailment. They believe that to do so would be to admit a weakness. Some women go to the other extreme of running to the doctor continually because they only have contact with their bad feelings. They will not permit themselves to feel good. I do not mean, however, to imply that men are always strong and women are always weak. I have also known many "strong" women who deny their feelings. I remember one client of mine who told me she refused to "give in" to sickness. When she got sick, whether with flu, a backache, or a heart attack, her normal behavior was to drive herself even harder. She remembered her mother telling her when she felt sick as a child, "You're not sick, you're only being lazy." Unfortunately, she could not tell that to her sick heart.

Let's face it, we all feel. We were all feeling babies who learned to turn off our feelings as we grew older. As grownups we need to give ourselves permission to do that which we did automatically so many years ago—to feel all our feelings, good and bad. If you have lost contact with your feelings, if you believe that you do not feel, start with the feelings you do know. Start with hunger or thirst, having to urinate, or becoming tired. Then go on from there. Explore your feelings through your bodily reactions.

I have heard many people ask, "What is a feeling?" My definition of a feeling is a subjective, sensual reaction to a stimulus or event. This reaction is physically manifested in your body. When I feel, I experience something within my own body, some reaction to what's going on outside of me or even to some remembered event in my own mind. I am aware of my feelings through my senses; I don't think them out in my head. I experience them throughout my body. In order to know what you are feeling, become aware of your body. Notice which muscles react when you experience anger, hurt, sadness, joy. You may stiffen your back with anger; you may ache with hurt in your stomach and feel sadness welling up in your head. Someone else may hold anger in his or her tightened arms; that person may fill his or her chest with joy. Each person has different physical reactions in his body; become aware of yours.

Become aware of your pain. We have been taught to distract ourselves from our pain in order to avoid feeling it. We have learned to clench our teeth against pain. "I can't feel that; it hurts too much," we say to ourselves. But the pain lingers on. We don't bury our feelings dead; we bury them alive within ourselves. To let the pain go we need to do the opposite—to feel it. When you feel your pain, pay attention to its physical manifestation within your body. Some people make the mistake of thinking about the situation which elicited their emotional response. They fantasize about what they should or should not have done, what they should have said. Their fantasizing only escalates their emotion. They end up stuck with their feelings because they have not allowed themselves to feel the pain attached to that original situation. To let the pain go, quit fantasizing. Pay attention to your body.

When I began to study Gestalt techniques I learned from my teacher (who learned from Fritz Perls), "Pain is a part of life. If you don't feel your pain, you're only half alive." Paradoxically, if you do not allow yourself to experience your original pain, you may feel it forever. I consider "half alive" synonymous with "chronic." Unfelt pain becomes a low-level, constant tension. Anger, unfelt, becomes guilt or ulcers or migraines. Tears, unshed, become sinusitis or chronic depression. Excitement, suppressed, becomes frigidity or boredom. Each unfelt pain may become some disguised but constant intruder.

Sometimes even sexual excitement can be attributed to unfelt pain. Steve W. started therapy because his marriage was failing. He attributed all his bad feelings to his marital situation. He complained that his wife rarely wanted to have sex with him. "It's driving me up the wall," he said. "All I can think of is sex, sex, sex. I have to masturbate two or three times a day so I won't go out of my mind." Then Steve got into some of his deep feelings about his mother. He went back in his feelings to when he was about three years old. He felt the pain of her rejection of him when his younger sister was born and the pain of his unsatisfied want and need. Steve sobbed and howled out his pain for over an hour. When he finished he felt high. He grinned at me. "I never knew I hurt so much when I was a kid," he said. "I wouldn't want to go through the last hour again but it was worth it. I feel free, somehow."

During the next session Steve shared his insights into his sexual tension with me. "I haven't wanted sex this past week the way I did before," he said. "I haven't been tense at all and haven't felt the need to masturbate. Mary and I finally got together and it was different—deeper, more tender. I can't describe it, really, but I know that I haven't itched to have sex. When we did have it, it seemed whole and more fulfilling than I've ever known. I know now my wanting sex so much is actually my wanting my mother with my whole being, and not having her when I was a kid."

Steve's insights did not save his marriage, nor did the one experience permanently alter his sexual needs. But each time he gets into his deep feelings he lets go more of his childhood need. He finds that the sexual encounters he does have become more meaningful as his sexual tension abates. I wondered after hearing of Steve's experience if men who brag about their machismo and their sexual prowess are merely more tense than others. Certainly women who are labelled "nymphomaniacs" must be acting out their tension sexually rather than attaining sexual fulfillment.

In the same way that Steve let his tension go by experiencing his original unfelt pain, you can let go of yours. Each time you contact your painful feelings you will release a little more tension. If you have controlled yourself so much that you have lost touch with your feelings, practice directing your attention toward them. Think of your attention as a magic wand. When you give your full attention to another person, that person feels recognized, validated, even healed by the power of your attention. You validate your own feelings, your existence, when you direct your attention into yourself. Become aware of when you are *directing* your attention and when you are dissipating it.

Your attention cannot be fully directed to more than one place at one time. You may think you can pay full attention to the radio, to your kids squabbling, and the book you are reading at the same time. Actually you cannot. You will not be focusing the full power of your attention on any one of those things. You will be paying rapid attention to each of them in turn but you will not be intensely aware of any of them. Learn to focus your attention fully on one thing at one time and you will find that you can concentrate on what you read, remember facts, and think clearly. You will become aware of when your attention is in your head (thinking) and when it is in your body (feeling). You will become aware of when your attention is on your own feelings and when you are focusing on someone else. And by becoming aware of where your attention is focused you may find out more quickly which people are good for you and whom you need to avoid.

Let your feelings tell you. If you are with someone who is comfortable to be with, you will no doubt feel relaxed, open, and expansive. Stay in touch with your own good feelings. You will receive many positive strokes and nurturing from someone with whom you feel comfortable. If you are with someone who is uncomfortable to be with, resist the urge to numb yourself to your own bad feelings. You will automatically want to listen and watch that person carefully. But when you place all your attention on someone with whom you feel uncomfortable, you lose touch with your own feelings. You may even lose the awareness that you feel scared, angry and full of pain around this person.

I have confused myself in the past by thinking that some people who were very uncomfortable to be with were fascinating because I was paying such close attention to them. I was fascinated in the same way a bird is transfixed by a snake. I made the very costly mistake of marrying such a person. I discovered later that when I was fascinated by his conversation I was thinking, "I can't converse as well"; by his intellect, "I'm not as smart"; by his activities, "I'll never do as much." By being fascinated with him and putting all my attention on him, I discounted myself. I would not have been confused by this person had I kept my attention on my own bad feelings. But I discounted my feelings with messages like "You shouldn't feel that way," "Give him a chance," and "Don't be silly." And I confused myself. I listened to the messages in my head, my own fantasies. I told myself to "behave" (whatever that is). Had I paid attention to my bad feelings instead, and recognized them as valid, I would have either avoided him, or expressed my feelings strongly (in which case, he would probably have avoided me).

So, stay open to your discomfort. Instead of paying such careful attention to that uncomfortable person, keep your attention on your own bad feelings; let yourself hurt. You may not change the other's behavior, but you will not put yourself down and you will let your bad feelings go more quickly. You may find that your tears pour out as you feel your pain; let them flow. At least you will not retain your pain. And if that person criticizes you for crying you have one more indication that he or she is pure poison for you. You will not stay around that person as long. Nor will you confuse yourself by thinking your fascination is love, as I did, and making your uncomfortable relationship more permanent.

When is the last time you allowed yourself to become aware of your feelings? Give yourself time now. Sit down in an easy chair or lie down. Relax. Get your attention off your fantasies and out of your head; put it into your body. Now let your attention wander throughout your body until it finds some point of tension, discomfort, or pain. When it finds that place, let your attention rest there. Let the pain or discomfort grow and become worse. Let it hurt you. Keep your attention on it as the pain gets bigger. Now let the pain change; let it go anywhere in your body that it wants to go. Just keep your attention on it as it moves around. You may encounter several points of pain in your body. Let your attention rest on each of them while they grow and change. Then let the pain go out of you. It may go out through the top of your head or your back or your finger tips. It may not leave entirely but remain in a diminished form. This exercise may take you a few minutes, or it may take a half an hour if you are full of pain and tension. At the end of the exercise you will probably find yourself more relaxed, free of much of the pain you had been holding in your body. You may even go to sleep. When I do this exercise in my classes people often go to sleep.

One man told me, "Your exercise didn't work. I slept through it."

"What do you feel now?" I asked him.

"Relaxed," he said.

"Thank you," I said. "I'm glad you enjoyed it."

If you believe that you cannot feel, you may not accept your feelings even while you are expressing them. Put another way, if your attention is on the "shoulds" in your head rather than on your feelings, you may not recognize your own feelings when you have them. One member of my group was given strong injunctions against feeling when she was a child. Her mother, moreover, had expressed such violent feelings that the girl decided she did not want to act like that. In group sessions she continually berated herself for not getting into her feelings. Invariably, as she criticized herself for not feeling, she would cry. When I asked her "What are you feeling?" she would say, "Nothing." She would not believe that her tears expressed her feelings; therefore, she did not believe she was feeling anything.

I am also aware that the harder you try to feel, the less you will feel. Trying hard means straining against yourself. When you strain to do anything you defeat yourself. I tried very hard to write my dissertation. I tried so hard I wrote it completely three times. Had I stopped trying so hard and just done it, I would have written it only once. When you try hard to feel you become numb. Try hard to relax and what happens? You become more tense. Try hard to do anything, for that matter, and you will find it more difficult to achieve. Alan Watts points out that it is your trying that defeats you: "When you try to stay on the surface of the water, you sink; but when you try to sink you float. When you hold your breath you lose it. . . ."*

I am convinced that trying hard is one of the most insidious and all-pervasive of the messages our parents have given us. If you are one who tries harder you will never know contentment. No matter what you do you will always tell yourself you could have tried harder and done more. You will take the hardest path when you could have taken the easiest and you will fight your own tension every step of the way. I know; I have tried hard most of my life. I remember having a dream that exemplified how hard I have tried. In the dream I rented a standard bike and started pedalling up a steep hill. I could feel my every muscle straining and my lungs aching as I struggled up the hill. Halfway up I had to get off the bike and stop. I was too tired to go any further. When I worked on the dream in a group I was attending the therapist asked me how I might rewrite the dream. "That's easy," I said. "I'd turn around and coast down the hill. Then I'd rent a five-speed bike." Later, when I told my husband about the experience, he said, "Why don't you rent a ten-speed bike and be done with it?" I gasped. Even in working through the dream I had chosen a bike with fewer gears so I could still try harder! (Today I'd pick a motorcycle!)

The only way to stop trying hard is to go ahead and do whatever you are doing. There is a difference between attempting something initially and trying harder. If you never take the risk of try-

*Alan Watts, *The Wisdom of Insecurity* (New York, Vintage Books, A Division of Random House, Inc., 1941), p. 9.

ing, you will never accomplish anything. But the harder you try the less you will accomplish. So quit trying hard. If what you are doing turns out well, you have done it without strain. If it turns out poorly, there is always a tomorrow when you can try again.

Only when you finally stop trying hard to feel and believing that you cannot feel, will you begin to get in touch with your feelings. You may also notice that your defenses seem to gain strength at first. Defenses are methods we use to avoid feeling our feelings; they can be behavior patterns as well as mental blockages against feeling. Call them self-manipulations, if that makes sense. When you begin to allow long unfelt emotions into your awareness, your particular defense may take over out of habit. Some people simply turn off feelings. Others light a cigarette, race for the cookie jar, or grab for their liquor, pills, or drugs. Other people talk, think, shop, laugh, work, read, or go crazy as a defense against their feelings. Whatever your particular defense, simply be aware of it, then allow yourself to feel your feelings. They won't last forever. If you experience pain, feel shaky, or become afraid, remember that you may be feeling an emotion related to an event from the past. If so, the situation no longer exists exactly as it was then, nor are the people in your memory the same as before. Furthermore, you do not have enough energy to sustain your feeling forever. Your painful feeling will pass when you run out of energy. So, go ahead and allow yourself to feel without using your defense. You will survive without it.

Watts points out that defense is impossible anyway:

> The pain is inescapable, and resistance as a defense only makes it worse; the whole system is jarred by the shock . . . To remain stable is to refrain from trying to separate yourself from a pain because you know that you cannot. Running away from fear is fear, fighting pain is pain, trying to be brave is being scared. If the mind is in pain, the mind is pain. The thinker has no other form than his thought. There is no escape.*

Once you stop using a defense against your feelings you will need to substitute a positive form of behavior in place of your old familiar habit. When you drop the old ways you create a vacuum. It is tempting to fill that vacuum with the behavior, feelings, and

*Watts, p. 97.

attitudes you already know instead of finding new ones. I remember when I rejected strokes as a defense against feeling good. Someone would say to me, "My, you look nice in that outfit." And I would return, "This old thing? Yes, I got it at a thriftship and the skirt is too short and there's this spot on the blouse and look at this awful lining. It only cost. . . ." I spent much of my time and conversation rejecting strokes. When I started to feel good enough about myself to accept strokes, I had to learn a whole new way of conversing. At first I would respond, "Thank you," to a stroke and stop, not knowing what to say next. It took time for me to learn to accept a stroke and still go on with the conversation.

Carol B., whom I mentioned earlier, told me that she and Walter had a similar problem changing their behavior patterns. She said that she used to spend several hours being angry with Walter, several fighting with him, several feeling bad, and several making up her mind to talk to him again. These activities sometimes filled not only one day but several. When they decided to relate on a feeling level, Carol and Walter were able to achieve intimacy. They could communicate their feelings directly to each other without all the destructive behavior they had engaged in before. Often they did not know what to do next. Nor did they know what to do with all their free time. At first they easily fell back into their old manipulations because they had not yet worked out more constructive activities with which to fill the hours in a day.

Even the complaining that many women do about their feelings may be regarded as a defense. They are filling time with the activity of talking. When they complain, they are not feeling their feelings; they are *talking about* them, which is very different from *feeling* them. They are also trying to convince their listener of how bad they feel and trying to get the listener to make them feel better. They are playing the old Victim game of "Do something for me because I am too helpless to do anything for myself." They say they are feeling depressed. But depression is not a feeling; it is a feelingless state. People become immobilized and listless from depression because they use all their energy to hold down their feelings. They simply have no energy left with which to move. If they would allow themselves to do the hurting they need to do, the depression would lift and their energy would return.

Perhaps the most important reason so many women become

severely depressed is that they have been given so many messages against expressing their anger. Our culture encourages women to be helpless and incompetent so that their heroes can support them. So women hold in their anger and smile helplessly, not daring to acknowledge their inner feelings to themselves, let alone anyone else. No woman can stuff herself with feelings without repercussions, for feelings do not go away by themselves. There has to be a backlash if the feelings remain unexpressed or unacknowledged. That backlash is often a chronic depression. Thousands of women complain of such depression to doctors, who may label it "menopause," at a loss for another diagnosis. In *The Secret Strength of Depression*, Frederic Flach discusses the relation of unexpressed feelings to depression:

> The exact point at which a chronic depression may have begun is hard to spot. Unlike acute depression, the chronic form is usually detached from its causes in the person's mind. Feelings which should have been experienced at the time of the stressful events may have been denied, blocked out. Sometimes people may even be misled into being "proud" of how calmly they seemed to have handled a particular misfortune. The importance of the causal events may escape notice because the person failed to become sufficiently upset by them at the time.*

I remember Ingrid M., who was in a state of extreme chronic depression, thinking of little else but suicide. Her husband, a navy pilot, had been killed in a plane crash almost two years before I met her. In the funeral ceremonies that followed his death she had not been permitted to cry. "I wanted to, at first," she said, "but every time I started to cry, someone would poke me or pinch me and say, 'Navy wives don't cry,' or 'Be brave for your husband's sake.' They kept shoving tranquilizers down me so I couldn't feel anything. After about five days of that I didn't feel any pain at all. And I haven't felt anything since. I still can't cry about it. All I want to do is kill myself." I had the feeling many times that Ingrid was proud of her wish to die as if she were daring someone, "Just try to stop me."

Fortunately for Ingrid, she had the unlimited resources of the

*Frederic Flach, *The Secret Strength of Depression* (New York, Bantam Books, J. B. Lippincott Edition, 1975), p. 7.

navy medical program behind her. She went to psychiatrists three times a week and was also given enormous quantities of antidepressants. In order to externalize her anger, her psychiatrist told her, she was to take it out on something other than herself. He suggested that every time she felt like killing herself she go outside and chop a limb off a tree. I thought that was a pretty good suggestion, albeit devastating for her trees. By the time she had chopped her way through all the trees in her yard and started on her neighbor's, she was able to try an alternative form of getting her anger out, beating on pillows.

The last few times I saw Ingrid she no longer wished to die. "I've found out that I was idealizing my husband," she said. "I no longer have to do that. I can admit the reality of my marriage and what my husband was, as well as the reality of my life now. I have done a lot of crying about his death and I'm about over it. I know I have a life I can look forward to and enjoy from here on."

Ingrid's burying of her feelings at the time of her husband's death caused her to become chronically depressed for over four years. Had she been allowed to do her grieving at the time, she would have gotten over it in a matter of months rather than years. She had indeed been brave, and she wasted several years of her life because of it. Ingrid is no longer brave or proud. She is alive.

All of us get depressed from time to time. Depression may be caused by a combination of painful events, repressed feelings, and parent messages (those damnable "shoulds"). In order to lift that depression, you need to feel the pain within your body, express your feelings if you are able, and get your attention out of your head. The more you listen to your "shoulds," the more depressed you will become. Put your attention into your senses instead. Some people may be able to put their total attention into their sense of hearing by listening to music. Others may be able to get out of their heads by tasting, smelling, or looking at something. My favorite method, however, is to use my sense of touch. When I begin to fantasize, or dwell on my "shoulds," I put my attention onto textures. You try it. Close your eyes so you will not start to think about what you feel. Now touch various textures. What do you feel inside your body as you touch wood, stone, plastic, fur, leaves, rubber, cloth, skin? My list could go on and on. How about yours? By feeling textures through your sense of touch you will stay out of your fantasies and in the here and now. And by breaking your habit of dwelling on your "shoulds" you may just keep your occasional down periods from becoming chronic depressions.

I am a firm believer in wallowing in feelings. If I feel bad, I go ahead and feel bad all the way. You should too; cry, wail, howl, let yourself get into the feeling with spirit. One client told me that her doctor suggested a method to help her cry even more when she felt badly. "Look in the mirror the way you used to do when you were a kid," he told her. "Watch yourself crying and it will help you feel worse." There's nothing wrong with feeling sorry for yourself because you feel so bad. You need to feel sorry for yourself occasionally. And while you're at it, take a permission that one of my groups worked out: "It's okay to feel bad without feeling bad about it." It is better to feel bad today than stay depressed for a hundred tomorrows!

You might be able to accept your feelings more easily if I could convince you that feelings are amoral—outside the strictures of morality. There is no right or wrong to feelings. They just are. You just feel. No one can tell you that you should not feel that way, just because you do. Muriel Schiffman, in *Gestalt Self Therapy*, says: *"There is no justice in human emotions.* Feelings are nonrational; the unconscious is illogical. . . . Justice, fairness, blame, are irrelevant issues when the other person is in the midst of an intense emotion."* It is okay to *feel* anything. It is okay to *think* anything. It is *not* okay to *do* anything because there is morality attached to action. Your actions may be labelled right or wrong by society. So you can feel like killing someone; you can think about killing someone, and it is okay. If you do kill someone, it is a wrongful act.

When I first started teaching these concepts several years ago, one of my class members, raised as a Catholic, had problems accepting what I was saying. "I was taught that I should be pure in thought, word, and deed," she said, "and to me that includes feelings." I explained that I had been taught the same doctrine and had bought it for many years until I realized that feelings—all of them—were okay. As in all my classes I emphasized that I did not expect that she should believe me, just that she consider what I was

*Muriel Schiffman, *Gestalt Self Therapy and Further Techniques for Personal Growth* (Menlo Park, Dist. by Bookpeople, Self Therapy Press, California, 1971), p. 77.

saying. Who am I to inflict any more "shoulds" on anybody? People usually have enough of their own! She came to the next session very relieved. "I heard a lecture by one of the most liberal priests in town," she said, "and he said that feelings and thoughts are okay. So I can stop going to confession for having bad thoughts and feelings and just stick to what I do. I sure won't have to go to confession as often!"

Accepting your feelings is not easy if you have been taught all your life that your feelings do not count. You may say to yourself, "It's okay to feel," but you will catch yourself saying familiar words to yourself: "I shouldn't be feeling this way"; "That's too petty to get mad about"; "I shouldn't be angry, he didn't mean it"; "There's nothing to be scared about"; or "It's silly to feel this way." The truth is that much of the time you may not really know why you feel what you do. You may not know until later; you may never know. But you feel and that is enough. Allow yourself to feel that way. Feelings are real facts inside our bodies. Feelings have cause, effect, and embodiment. Feelings are.

If someone asks you to explain or justify your feelings, don't think you have to answer. "Why are you feeling that way?" may not merit an explanation if you are not sure yourself. All you have to do is keep validating your feelings. "I don't know, but I am—" (fill in sad, angry, happy, or whatever you are feeling). You have a right to your feelings. No matter what they are, they are yours and they are okay. You are not wrong or crazy for feeling what you do, though many in our culture will try to convince you that you are.

Many children are raised in "crazy-making" families, which on first impression seem to be very nurturing families. But the "shoulds" and "don'ts" add up in the child's mind to "Don't feel what you feel; feel what I tell you to feel," and, "Don't think what you think; think what I tell you to think." Soon the child will be confused, thinking, "I know what I'm feeling, but Mom and Dad say I shouldn't be feeling that, so I'm wrong to feel that way," or, "I must be crazy to think that!" So the child turns off the feelings. I have heard similar descriptions of crazy-making messages in marriage situations. "He keeps telling me I shouldn't be feeling the way I do," one wife told me. "To tell the truth I don't know what I feel anymore. I'm going nuts."

One client of mine could not understand why she had such

negative feelings about her parents and her early childhood until she uncovered some of the crazy-making messages she had received. Rescuing was standard fare, "There, there, don't cry, it'll all go away." This woman reported feeling terribly apprehensive if she felt the least bit angry. "After all," she said, "what right had I to get mad when my parents tried so hard to make me happy?" Not only that, the whole family regarded any forceful expression of feeling as the equivalent of craziness. My client interpreted many of their messages to her as "You're crazy to feel that way," with the result that she did develop an overwhelming fear of going crazy. Before she came into my group she committed herself to a psychiatric hospital for three months because she believed she was indeed crazy.

Another client only remembered the love her parents had given her when she was a child. She firmly believed that she had been happy then. Her parents had told her many times over the years what a perfect daughter she was. She managed to live up to these expectations until she graduated from college. Then she developed a phobia. She became afraid of spiders and professed disgust at seeing their webs. She began to spend several hours each day searching for cobwebs, cleaning her apartment, and washing her hands after she thought she had touched a web. She believed she was crazy for acting so compulsively but did not know how to stop.

Through therapy she began to see that the parents she had believed were all loving were in reality extremely controlling. She understood that she had become terrified of failing to live up to the perfect ideal they expected. Her fear of losing their love if she failed at anything, plus her decision to split off from her real feelings by adapting to their expectations, added up to a tremendous load of internal fear, hurt, and anger. Since she could see no reasons for these feelings, she transferred them onto something which seemed to her to make sense—spiders. Once she learned to direct her anger appropriately toward the parents of her childhood, she stopped harassing her eight-footed friends. She stopped defending against her feelings by compulsive behavior and allowed herself to feel her previously denied "crazy" feelings toward her parents.

Claude Steiner gives a clear description of crazy-making messages and how to deal with them in *Scripts People Live*. Steiner uses the word "accounting" to describe how one may express one's feelings to another: ". . . people who are frequently discounted, and come to experience the disorientation and perhaps the eventual madness that is the result of discounts, need to learn the antithesis to the discount which I called Accounting, and to deal with power plays."* Sometimes another person may not permit you to account for your feelings or to communicate in any way. That person may walk out and slam the door behind him or her leaving you talking to the door. In such a case it does you little good to talk to the person who is no longer there. But you can still validate your feelings by becoming aware of them. Describe to yourself what is happening in your body so you know what you're feeling. Talk out loud if you need to. You may not be able to tell anyone what you feel but at least you won't be entirely stuck with your feelings.

You may also communicate what you're feeling to another person in this way. A woman jumped on me recently with a load of accusations. I was caught unaware and could feel myself getting upset. As she listed her angry complaints I simply reported my feelings: "I'm really upset about what you're saying"; "I'm irritated at you for saying that"; "I'm angry at you for not telling me all this before"; and "I'm so angry I'm shaking." When I reported that, she stopped and said, "Well, that's your problem" and strode off. She was right; it was my problem, my feelings. There was no solution to this argument. I hadn't made her feel bad, as she accused me of doing. I could not make her feel better; I didn't try. I simply reported what I was feeling. Afterwards, I didn't feel exactly elated because it was a no-win confrontation that resolved nothing. But I did feel good because I had not defended myself. I did not accuse and I got rid of my feelings as I felt them. I shook for about fifteen minutes, as I usually do after having an upsetting encounter, yet felt centered and solid.

You may not win all your arguments if you express your feelings. You will still meet people who project their internal load of anger onto you, as the woman I just described did to me. There are a lot of angry people in this world. You cannot avoid them. But you can stay straight with yourself. You can get your feelings out of your own body so that you are not stuck with them mentally, as

---

*Claude Steiner, *Scripts People Live: Transactional Analysis of Life Scripts* (New York, Grove Press, 1975), p. 280.

grudges, or physically, as psychosomatic complaints. And you have more of a chance of having the other person hear you than if you defend yourself or accuse, both of which tend to escalate the other person's anger.

You can also hear others. The most important thing I have to say to you is to validate feelings, yours and others! If you get nothing else out of this book, learn to quit rescuing. Just as you permit yourself to have feelings, permit others too. Rather than discounting, ignoring, or criticizing the feelings of others, recognize them. You cannot make others' feelings go away by telling them they "should." You cannot make them feel better if they do not choose to. "When in doubt, stroke," is a good maxim to remember. Stroke other people's feelings by being aware of them and expressing your awareness to those people. When your children cry, instead of saying "Don't cry," say something like "You're really unhappy, aren't you?" When they express fear, quit telling them "There's nothing to be afraid of." You may not think so, but they do. Say, for example, "You sound like you're really scared." If they get angry at you and say "I hate you," quit telling them they're bad to say that. Allow them to express their anger. Say, "I hear you," or "I don't blame you for hating me," or "Okay." Give them permission to feel. Give the same permission to your spouse, your relatives, your friends. The permission I often express is, "It's okay to get angry with me and tell me about it—just no hitting. I bruise easily." Control your dog, make him obey, but allow your people to feel.

You don't have to take responsibility for the feelings of others. You can allow them to be as they are. Once you stop taking responsibility for another's feelings you will hurt much less, and lose a great deal of your anger. I remember one time when I was vividly aware I had quit taking responsibility for feelings. I was late to teach an evening class and hurriedly backed my car out of the driveway. I completely forgot about the wire fence my husband had rigged to keep in the dog. When I realized I had backed through the fence, I drove back down into the yard, compounding the damage by dragging the fence with me. I went into the house to tell my husband and he exploded. We went out together to fix the fence and he swore all the time we were doing it. I was thinking, "Is he ever mad! I don't blame him; I'd be mad too. That fence is a wreck. Wow, he's even using words I haven't heard before!" But I was not anxious and I did not feel wrong. In fact, I felt good because I allowed him to express his feelings without defending myself against them. And he felt okay because he got rid of his anger. By the time we got the fence fixed the air between us was clear again.

You can allow yourself to be who you are as well. Accept yourself as you are feeling in the here and now. You will begin to respond to what is happening now, rather than to the messages in your head from the past. The late Fritz Perls said:

> . . .this is what I hope to do . . . to make you understand how much you gain by taking responsibility for every emotion, every movement you make, every thought you have—and shed responsibility for *anybody* else. . . . Responsibility, in one context, is the idea of obligation. If I take responsibility for somebody else, I feel omnipotent: I have to interfere with his life. . . . But responsibility can also be spelled response-ability: the ability to respond, to have thoughts, reactions, emotions in a certain situation. . . . Responsibility means simply to be willing to say "I am I" and "I am what I am" . . .*

Recognize how many of your own feelings you project onto others. Events that occur in the present certainly activate our feelings, but much of what we feel is made up of what Perls calls "unfinished business" from the past. So we project our feelings onto the present situation and believe it is that situation which "makes" us feel. For example, you may look outside at the rain and say, "That rain makes me sad." In reality, the rain is only bringing into your conscious awareness your internal feelings of sadness. Or, you may criticize a woman for flaunting her sexuality. Your projection here is probably your own repressed sexual feelings flashing into awareness. Or, you may feel lost and lonely when you read about an orphaned child. Here your feelings of abandonment and loneliness may be coming up to awareness.

Projection is like a cord that stretches between you and the person or thing onto which you are projecting. Cut the cord and you take back the projection; you own it; you become responsible for it. Perls says:

---

*Frederic S. Perls, M.D., Ph.D., *Gestalt Theory Verbatim* (New York, Bantam Books, Real People Press, 1974), pp. 69–70.

> We are not willing to take the responsibility that we are critical, so
> we project criticism onto others. We don't want to take the responsi-
> bility for being discriminating, so we project it outside and then we
> live in eternal demands to be accepted, or the fear of being rejected.
> And one of the most important responsibilities—this is a *very* impor-
> tant transition—is to take responsibility for our projections, re-
> identify with these projections, and become what we project.*

To become what you project in the above examples, go into the rain.
Become the rain and imagine that you are falling down onto the
earth. See what you feel as the rain. Or, become the woman as she
walks along the street. Allow yourself to feel the sexual feelings you
assign to her. See what you feel as you flaunt your sexiness. Or,
become an orphaned child. Imagine what you would feel without
either parent, what you would do. Become the child. Go into whatever feeling or behavior you are ascribing to other people or things
and you may discover some surprising feelings within yourself. It is
often easier to see in others that which we will not see in ourselves.
This is particularly evident to me when I work with couples.

Betty and Karl M. were both projecting their inner feelings
onto each other when they came to me. In our first session together
Karl did all the talking while Betty listened. Karl blamed their
problems on her relatives. He felt excluded and criticized by her
family. He said she told her family everything but would not talk to
him. I asked if they had any other problems with their marital
relationship. He said, "No, just her dependency on her family."
When I asked her what she felt, she hesitated and again he started
talking. I asked him to let her speak and she finally blurted out that
she felt put down, criticized, and restricted. He was surprised by
this but later admitted that she had good cause to feel that way; he
said he knew now that he had restricted her activities when they
had first gotten married. I explained to them that a marital problem
is never one-sided. If he had restricted her, she had allowed herself
to be treated that way without expressing her feelings to him. If she
would not communicate with him, it might be his behavior that was

*Perls, p. 70.

partially to blame. I had the feeling that neither believed me. Each insisted that their problems were entirely the other's fault.

We had many sessions after that. Karl said that he wanted the marriage to succeed because he loved Betty and he wanted no one else as his wife. Betty did not share Karl's feelings. She wanted to stay married because she was afraid she could not make it on her own. Even though the couple had no children Betty was afraid of having to support herself. In her dependency on Karl, Betty saw him as father figure, breadwinner, and her severest critic. Betty eventually stopped working for the relationship and wanted to separate. She told Karl to leave half a dozen times. Each time he left she would get scared that she could not make it alone and ask him to come back.

Although Karl had never hit Betty, she expressed fear that he might. She was also terrified when they argued and he raised his voice. She said that these were the reasons she never talked back to him or expressed her anger.

"What did you feel about your father?" I asked.

"Oh, my father," she moaned. "He terrified me. When he would get angry at me he would yell and yell and yell. He rarely hit me but sometimes I prayed that he would; his yelling was more terrible than spankings. When he hit me, then it was over, but when he screamed at me I could hear it in my ears for days after. I felt more anxious about what he might do than what he actually did! And, I could never do anything right for him. He had to approve of whatever I did or wherever I went. If he didn't approve, whatever I wanted was out. I guess I thought he was God. He did too," she added.

"Did he ever compliment you for anything?" I asked.

Betty thought for a long while. "No," she answered, "I don't think he did. He wanted me to study hard and get good grades but he never praised me when I got them. It was always, 'You can get better grades in your other subjects too if you work harder.' He wanted me to be a success. He said all of our family had always been successful so I had better be too. If I failed I would shame the family, he said."

"And were you successful?" I asked.

"No, not at all," she said. "I was too scared about failing to even try. I didn't start college because I knew I wouldn't make it through and I would shame my father. And now I'm afraid to go out and get a job because I know I won't be able to do it. That's why I need Karl; I just can't support myself on my own."

As we worked more on her feelings and memories about her father, Betty began to understand that she had projected many of her feelings about him onto Karl. She was terrified of Karl's anger, not because he had ever hurt her but because she thought he might, like she had feared her father might. She expected his criticism as she had her father's, and when he did criticize her, she resented him. The more fearful and angry she became, the more she turned to her mother and to her sisters for solace. And the more excluded Karl felt.

"Did you ever feel excluded as a child?" I asked Karl.

"All the time," he said. "I was an only child of foreign-born parents. I didn't speak English very well when I was small so the other kids kidded me about my speech. I guess I was kind of a scapegoat. They kidded me about my folks the most. Once a bunch of them beat me up because I was different. That was the only reason, just that I was different. My folks never did understand what I was going through. They had enough to cope with, being new in this country and out of work most of the time. They expected me to handle my problems. I never felt that I belonged anywhere but I couldn't do anything about it. And I couldn't ask my parents for help. They had their own problems.

"What were their problems?" I asked.

"Well, besides the problems involved in changing cultures and earning a living, they didn't get along very well. My father was of the old school. He believed a wife should take care of the home and the children and leave the rest to the men. He didn't like her going out of the home at all, and when she tried, he'd put his foot down. She never really crossed him but she resented him. She griped a lot to me."

Through therapy, Karl was able to understand that he was treating Betty as his father had treated his mother. He did not like his father's actions, but he had no other example to follow, so he acted in similar ways. The more he tried to control Betty's behavior, the more she resented him. Then, instead of telling him about her feelings, she turned to others for consolation and Karl would feel more of his childhood feelings of exclusion.

The last time I saw Betty she had once again told Karl to leave. This time she filed for divorce; she was determined not to ask him back. Perhaps in so doing she was taking the first step in severing her symbiotic bond with her father. Time will tell. If Betty has not gotten out of her symbiosis her next partner may resemble her father even more than Karl did. She may find herself tied to a perfectionist who does beat her. On the other hand, if Betty has indeed split the symbiosis and become aware of her projections, she may find someone to whom she can relate on a mature level instead of the child-to-parent relationship she had with Karl. She will be able to support herself. She will also recognize her projections from the past before they settle in to haunt her. She will be free of the painful, manipulative relationships that she had known before.

Karl too may break his symbiotic bond. He may be able to change his behavior and allow his future partner to be herself without any rigid expectations on his part. He may discover that he can act in a new way, different from his father, because he is himself and is not really like his parent. If he succeeds in changing his behavior and relates to his new partner without expectations, he may find that she includes him in her circle of confidants and expresses her feelings to him. And he may finally replace his projection of being excluded with a new feeling of belonging.

It hurts you to project your feelings onto others; you are dealing with unresolved feelings from years ago but confusing yourself about their origins. It also hurts to have others project their feeling onto you. I used to accept others' projections because I did not realize what they were doing. I did a lot of hurting because I believed I was "making them" feel one way or the other. It took me years to acquire insight. I remember "buying" a projection at one workshop on Transactional Analysis that I attended years ago. A workshop member turned to me and said fiercely, "You are a very angry lady." I was stunned. What had I said? I had done nothing of which I was aware. The workshop leader picked up on the transaction immediately.

"Are you aware of your anger?" she asked me.

"I think so," I responded. "I still have a lot of anger inside me towards my parents."

"What do you do with it when you feel your anger?" she asked.

"I pound a pillow or stamp my feet or throw a bean bag. Sometimes I scream a lot when I'm driving on the freeway," I responded.

She turned to the man who had confronted me and asked him similar questions. He was not aware of his anger, except toward me. The leader began to work with him. Through his work he discovered that he was indeed very angry at his mother. He got nothing but negative strokes and discounts from her. And since he had not realized the depth of his anger towards his mother, he had never connected where his anger was coming from with the situation which provoked his anger. He projected it instead onto other people.

I learned a great deal from that encounter. I began to suspect that some part of me of which I was unaware had activated this man's outburst. Maybe it did; maybe it did not. I could have been wearing a blue dress that reminded him of his mother; that alone could have inspired his angry outburst. Nevertheless, I knew I had work to do on my own growth because I had felt so defensive. I also discovered that I did not have to buy his projection wholeheartedly. I could hear his anger without forgetting I was not the sole source for his feeling. He had carried his load of anger a long time before he met me. He simply displaced that inner feeling onto me because my being there stirred something inside of him.

Once I learned about projections I became a more effective therapist. I learned to direct a client toward the source of his or her feeling. When a group member gets angry at me now, I no longer think, "What have I done?" as I used to do. Instead I think, "What is that person's projection?" I am aware that something about my being there activated his or her anger. It may have been something I did or said. It may have been a certain expression on my face or the tone of my voice. I know that I don't have to defend myself against these projections anymore. I can survive someone's expressing anger to me. But I also need to deal with whatever is happening in the here and now. The primary issue is where did the feelings come from in the original situation and who were they directed toward? But sometimes of equal importance is what is going on now to activate those feelings. For although we project many of our past feelings onto the present, the events that activate our feelings today are often the ones we need to clarify. When I try to analyze or interpret someone I often confuse myself and everybody else. I am fantasizing, which does not help the other person gain understanding. When I share my feelings about what is happening in the here and now, that person may more easily resolve his or her own problem, feeling better in the process.

I remember the other morning when I was rushing to help my little girl get ready for school—making her lunch, brushing her hair, getting her clothes out of the dryer. She was in an uncooperative mood and the more she dragged her feet the more rushed I felt.

"Why are you angry, Mommy?" she asked apprehensively.

"I'm not angry," I said. Then I checked my feelings. "I guess I am angry," I said. "I'm angry because you aren't helping me and we're going to be late getting you to school."

"See?" she said accusingly, and felt better.

I have learned to check my stomach to find out what I am feeling. I use it as my barometer, since my feelings are first discernible to me there. If my barometer starts to knot up, I say, "What's going on?" The knot in my stomach may answer, "I'm really excited," or a hollow emptiness may say, "I'm scared." When I know from my barometer what I'm feeling, I'm able to respond more appropriately to another person. I am also able to spot manipulations more quickly and recognize my own tendencies to join in. Then I can stop myself before I get into the game, either saying nothing (which often keeps me out of the Rescue Game) or expressing my feelings as straightforwardly as I can.

I have learned that I do not have to accept anger as my due from people, such as the woman who unleashed her pent-up rage on me. After mentally going over the scene I understood that she was projecting her feelings onto me only because I was there. I served as a convenient scapegoat upon whom she could heap all of her repressed anger. Her accusations about all the things I had done were irrational fantasies having little to do with actual events. Understanding her outburst as a projection, I was able to call it her problem and let it go at that. In a way, such a projection is "phony anger," rather than real anger—phony because her response was based on messages and feelings from her childhood. This woman had "shoulds" and "should nots" in her head that escalated her feeling. She was responding to her own fantasies and past experiences rather than the realities of the here and now. So her anger was generated by her thought processes and her repressed feelings and was not a straight, gut-level response toward me in the present.

When I think about it, I realize that we often respond with phony feelings in the sense that our responses are based on our projections. I understand Perls' meaning of "response-able" in this way. Children respond to others with gut-level feelings based on what is going on in the present. The older we get, the more we respond to other people with a lifetime's accumulation of garbage from the past. Our task, then, is to let go of the garbage, get in touch with our real feelings again, and respond to the here and now with the honesty of the feeling children we once were.

There are many ways to do this. Some people can achieve insight through reading a book; others can hear a lecture and reach some awareness. Most people, however, cannot get into deep awareness of their feelings by themselves. They need to work with someone who is skilled at helping people reach their feelings. Fortunately, there are innumerable opportunities today to do this kind of work. As a culture we are becoming aware of the need to express our feelings. Throughout America you can find therapists, groups, and associations devoted to helping you get in touch with your feeling self. So go to a workshop, get into group therapy, attend a marathon, or go to a retreat. Pick one that uses some form of feeling therapy: Gestalt, Bio-energetics, dance or play therapy, breathing or body work. If you go through a therapy that uses only words you may spend years talking about your feelings but never really feeling them. You may gain intellectual insight into your problems but still feel bad. So, if you are ready, get into your feelings instead. By feeling them you will let them go and be yourself in the here and now, unhindered by ghosts from the past.

In one workshop on Transactional Analysis I learned, "You can think your way to new feelings; you can act your way to new feelings." I would agree with this statement only up to a point. You can certainly change your attitudes along with your belief system and, as a result, have new feelings. You can modify your behavior in some ways to gain different feelings. But you may not be able to change your core feelings, those painful feelings from your earliest years. Sometimes, even when you believe you have worked through all your painful experiences in therapy, you still have occasional hints of pain buried deep inside your body. You may have dredged into all the painful feelings in your memory and cried them out. Still, you are aware of some vague hurt or anxiety. You wake up one morning feeling terrified. Or, you keep crying for no reason that you can identify. Or, you hold onto a defense which is destructive for you and you cannot seem to let it go. My understanding of these deep feelings is that they go back even farther than most of us care to admit. If you have studied Transactional Analysis you know of Eric Berne's diagram of the Parent-Adult-Child. Berne calls these ego states, "phenomenological realities," considering them not only theoretical concepts but living realities inside our brains. Berne illustrates the diagram of the P-A-C by a case history of a patient who

> exhibited three different ego states. These were distinguished by differences in her posture, manner, facial expression, and other physical characteristics. The first was characterized by tittering coyness, quite reminiscent of a little girl at a certain age; the second was primly righteous, like that of a schoolgirl almost caught in some sexual peccadillo; in the third, she was able to answer questions like the grown-up woman that she was.*

I have discovered, through working with many clients in therapy, that we can reach an ego level beyond Berne's "little girl," beyond the Child. We can reach our baby feelings. And, in therapy, the path to baby feelings is through feelings themselves, not through words or memories of events. As babies we could not verbalize our pain. Nor could we understand words that might have helped us through painful situations. Therefore, in a therapy which uses words as the only therapeutic process, clients may never be able to let go the core feelings which cause their pain. Still, they may be acutely aware of those painful and terrifying feelings. One

*Eric Berne, *Transactional Analysis in Psychotherapy: A Systematic Individual & Social Psychiatry* (New York, Ballantine Books, Grove Press, Random House, 1961), pp. 4, 10.

woman said, during a therapy session, "I was so split it feels strange to be *almost* one person. (I was four people: a crying baby, a little girl, the functioning me, and a me watching the other three.)"*

Corresponding to this woman's description, I believe that a more pertinent diagram than Berne's would be drawn showing four ego states, thus:

P Parent: containing message from your actual parents or parent figures, your internal "shoulds"

A Adult: containing your decision making, information-gathering, functioning in the Now, Self

C Child: containing your toddler feelings and memories from about two through childhood

B Baby: containing your baby feelings, birth to about two years of age

There are many therapies in use today which have various tools for helping you get in touch with your Self. Every therapist has his or her own way of working, sometimes combining several therapies in what is called an "eclectic" approach. One might say there are as many therapies as there are therapists. Growing numbers of therapists, recognizing a difference between Child and Baby feelings, are using techniques to get people past their verbal memories and into core feelings from their earliest years, even the birth experience itself.

Hypnotism is also an effective tool for modifying behavior, relaxing, letting go of pain, and sometimes even getting back into Baby feelings. If you can relinquish your control and allow yourself to be hypnotised, you may find a shortcut to breaking some of your destructive habits. You may not be able to get rid of all core feelings or let go those defenses which are still useful to you. But for many people hypnotism is a viable alternative to a more prolonged kind of therapy.

The most important thing to do, after you decide you are ready

*Arthur Janov, *The Primal Revolution* (New York, A Touchstone Book, Simon & Schuster, 1972), p. 240.

to work on your feelings, is to start. Therapy today is becoming increasingly accepted in our society. You need not be embarrassed about working on your problems, whatever they may be. Therapy is a learning process not unlike attending school. You learn to contact your feelings. You learn new theories to alter your belief system and how to modify your behavior. What can be more educational than that? You do not have to be "sick" to go into therapy; you may simply want some new growth techniques. If you do think you have emotional problems, remember that you have gotten to where you are today because of your innate desire to survive. Whatever defense you have used has had a purpose. However bizarre your defenses are, they have helped you cope with your life. Even craziness for some may be the safest and most appropriate way of responding to an otherwise intolerable situation.

Pick a therapist with whom you feel comfortable; you can check your feelings to find out if you do. If you don't trust one therapist, find someone else. You may need to shop around for someone you can work with. Or go to a lecture, class, workshop, or whatever to work on your own growth. If you are terrified at the thought of "getting into your feelings," if you are ready to expose yourself only through words, then stay with where you are. You may have to talk about your feelings for awhile before you're ready to risk feeling them—and that's okay! But start—somewhere—anywhere.

Now let us say that you have taken this initial step; you are working in depth on your feelings, whether or not you are going clear back to infancy. You are gaining insight into your parent messages and are substituting messages giving you permission to exist as yourself. You are connecting up some of your childhood experiences and how you've felt because of them. You are letting go the painful feelings you have had since childhood. You are beginning to understand how you defend against feeling and you're dropping those defenses. You are getting in touch with the feelings behind your projections, and you are no longer buying the projections of others.

There is one more thing you must do to feel okay about yourself. You need to accept yourself as you are right here, right now, regardless of what your life has been like before now. You could be in therapy for the next hundred years, and if you did not accept yourself as you are today, you would be miserable. So, sooner or later, no matter how much work you do on your own growth, you get down to the point of last resistance. At that point you need to accept yourself as you feel at that moment—every rotten, angry, sad, painful, lonely, and scared feeling, along with the good ones. Sooner or later you need to accept your past as history and let it all go—your mistakes, your failures, and your inappropriate behavior. You cannot relive your past. You cannot change history. Sooner or later, you need to be able to say to yourself, "I'm okay as I am right now, regardless of what has happened to me before today." You can say to yourself, "I am what I am and I am okay, not only in spite of my history, but because of it!"

You cannot go back to yesterday, nor can you reach tomorrow until it arrives. No matter who you are, you cannot guarantee the future. So you need to stop using your fantasies of the future to keep you from accepting the Now. Let it come as it will; you are still worthwhile. It does you no good at all to seduce yourself with promises that you'll be okay as soon as you get through therapy or you get a job or the kids leave home or you get a divorce, or any of the other excuses with which you and I deceive ourselves. Say instead, "I'm okay this minute and I'll be okay tomorrow no matter what!"

If you are waiting to accept yourself until you get through working on your growth, you are going to wait a long time. Going through therapy or working through problems does not mean that you will be free of pain and problems forever. Those you think are the most "together" people in the whole world still have their share of both. Problems are a part of life, just as your pain is a sign that you are still alive. One woman said to me recently, "How come, when I've been in therapy so long, I hurt so much?" I didn't know how to answer her, other than to congratulate her for allowing herself to hurt. Of course you will hurt. Being a feeling person means you hurt *more* when you encounter problems, that you are free then to feel your own pain. And when you feel it, you let it go. You are free to feel joy. So accept yourself for whatever you are feeling—good, bad, up, down, joyous, or full of pain. You are okay, no matter what you are feeling. And because you feel, you can experience the fullness of being alive.

Conclusion

The masks we assume as our disguises serve useful purposes. No wonder we take them off with such reluctance! Our masks establish our identities quickly by indicating the roles we play. They surround us with impenetrable walls. They protect us from the pangs of intimacy and prevent us from encountering our internal pain. They are our defense against feeling. Masks become polished and hardened after years of wear, more a part of us the older we get. They mold themselves to us with limpetlike strength. And we must mold ourselves to them. Our masks become our self-images.

Our masks have helped us get where we are today. They are a part of our history. We assumed our masks as we grew out of childhood, out of a state of dependence on those around us. When we reached adolescence, we learned that we could be independent of our parents but we fixed our masks even firmer. We wore them awkwardly, however, and with discomfort because they retained many of the features of our parents. They also hurt, preserving as they did our symbiotic bonds. As we grow into maturity we realize that we may discard our masks and become ourselves. We begin to understand that total independence is isolation; we do not want that. So we grow to interdependence with others. Maskless, we may bare our inner selves to others with all our imperfections and pain.

When we take off our masks and reveal ourselves to the world, we are naked and defenseless. We respond to events as they happen without attempting to control their outcomes. Neither do we attempt to control people. We allow them to see us as we really are; we do not need to defend ourselves. We see others as they really are, and we do not expect them to be other than they are. When we are hurt, we cry; when we are angry, we yell it out. We throw away our labels with our masks; we are no longer "nice" or "ladylike" or "gentlemanly." We are what we are when and where we are.

Some of us may be unwilling to take off our masks because of the pain involved. So we hide behind our particular disguise regardless of the cost to our own insides or to others around us. No one else can yank off our masks; no one has the power to force anyone else to feel. Each of us must make the decision; no one can make it for us. Each of us knows our own readiness to feel. If you are not ready, no one else can force you to feel. You cannot *force* yourself. But somewhere inside of you, you know when you can drop your defenses. Inside of you, you know when you will survive feeling your pain. If you have doubts that you will survive, if you are still blaming others for what you feel, if you will not recognize the origins of your feelings, then you are not quite ready to realize the depth of your pain.

So keep your mask on. I would not try to take it off for the world. Nor could I. In that particular tug of war you would surely win. It would be like trying to pick someone up who was severely depressed. I remember doing a demonstration in workshop once to illustrate depression. I played a depressed person, sitting limply on the floor. A 6′ man did his best to pick up my 5′2″ frame, but I kept slipping out of his grasp. We both ended up on the floor in a heap; I had pulled him down with my passivity. Depression is a mask that exhausts both the depressed person and the would-be Rescuer. Only the person who is motivated can get up the energy to take off his or her own mask.

No one else can supply your motivation. Motivation comes from your personal decision to change. Without that decision others are powerless to help. Perhaps you question your motivation; I do not. I know you have taken the first step in your quest for growth. You have read this book on self-growth and undoubtedly will read others. You are actively seeking change, whether or not you realize it. So, I will tell you the same thing I tell my class members—because you want to change and are willing to ask for help, you are already halfway there. "Where?" you ask me, "where am I halfway to?" Why, to your feeling Self, of course. Now all you have to do is to keep going—keep growing—keep allowing yourself to feel.

There are many people who do not think they need to change. They blame everyone else in the world for making them feel bad. They do not perceive others as they are in the Now. They are aware only of their fantasies. They are not willing to read a book on growth or take a class or go to a therapist. These are truly the people with problems. They are powerless to change because they take no responsibility for their feelings. And they are very uncomfortable to be around. They resist change in others. They want no part of growth. If you are stuck with such a person as a relative, friend, or neighbor, that person will try to prevent you from changing. You might have to make some hard decisions between going back to be what that person wants you to be, or continuing your growth.

It is not easy to grow, and it is not constant. Growth is never straight up. Sometimes you will level off and stay on the same plateau for what seems like an eternity. Sometimes you will go down again. Growth happens in spurts and in stages. If you miss a stage you may need to go back through it later in life. I know some people who have gone back to relive adolescence, even infancy, in their thirties and forties. The object of growing is to reach maturity but that is a state which we never attain completely. For growth is always toward an ideal and is never finished. Growth cannot be perfect while we are alive. If we attained full maturity we would stagnate and rot like an overripe apple. I want to keep growing, to never be done, because when I am finished I will be overripe, fallen on the ground, dead.

I know that the more I allow myself to grow, the more open I can be about my feelings. The more open I can be, the better I feel about myself. And the more worthwhile I feel the more I can reveal myself as I am in the here and now. When I used to feel very inferior I revealed little about myself. When I first started to feel okay I revealed a little more, but most of what I revealed was in the past. I remember when I first started doing groups five years ago I revealed a lot of past information, for example, "I thought I was going crazy a few years ago when I was married before." The more integrated I felt, the closer I was able to get to the Now, "I was depressed a few months ago when I couldn't find a full-time teaching job." Today I am usually able to share my feelings in the Now, "I am angry at you for what you're doing," or "I really freaked out over the weekend and I want to tell you about it." How about that? The more open I get the less perfect I have to be. No cast-iron image any more, just Me—less rigidity, more response.

I have found that the more I accept myself and the way I feel, the more awareness I have of my feelings. When I don't allow myself to be in touch with my feelings or when I barrage myself with "shoulds," I numb my body. It is then that I am unable to express my feelings to other people because I don't know what they are. All I can feel then is a general state of misery; I retain all my feelings in my body. I have numbed myself so much at times that I've given myself a stiff neck, a sore back, a headache, or a stomachache. Frankly, I would rather feel my feelings at the time than be stuck with a tense and hurting body for weeks afterwards.

I would rather grow and change. For although change may cause agitation in my relationships, I would rather have stress than stagnation. I would rather have the pain of experiencing my archaic childhood feelings than the muted misery of chronic, low-key depression. Growth is not as perceptible as having a tooth filled or a broken leg set. Growth, particularly in oneself, is usually discernable only in retrospect. And, because growth is so slow, painful, and hard to perceive, I believe the most important attribute one can have, besides the motivation to grow at all, is hanging-in-there, teeth-gritting, bulldog determination.

I have gritted my teeth and stumbled on, maturing despite myself. I didn't grow because I wanted to go through all that pain and effort; I grew because I was too miserable *not* to. I was terrified of feelings at first; it took me three years to get up the courage to go to a marathon. Feelings were foreign to me because I did not have permission to express all my feelings as a child. I had to learn that expressing anger and crying and being silly and feeling helpless were okay. Children who are raised with permission to express their feelings will have no problem knowing *what* they feel. By accepting their feelings they will be able to act in accordance with them. But I, like others without permission to feel, have had to analyze, probe, and dissect. I have had to gain an intellectual understanding of feelings in order to recognize them in my body. I have had to give myself conscious permission to act on my feelings and to express them.

Why else do you think I wrote this book? Or, for that matter, why else did I become a therapist? Because I have done so much thinking about feelings in order to know what they are and to know what I'm feeling! Because I have consciously, deliberately, let my misery go in order to achieve a sense of integration, of being Me. Perhaps I am most efficient as a therapist when I recognize a feeling in a client that I have known and dealt with. "Feeling a little paranoid today?" I might ask. "Yes, how did you know?" the client answers. "It takes one to know one," I reply.

I can look back at myself ten years ago and see a different person than I am today. I barely recognize that other me, now that I think about her. Change is so slow. Occasionally I have been aware at the time that I was feeling or acting differently than I had before. But most of the time I have changed at a snail's pace, only recognizing that change after the fact. Others, however, have become aware of my changing. I have lost some friends because they did not like my being straight with my feelings. I have not received much encouragement. Nobody (especially among those closest to me) has given me pats on the back and said, "Gee, thanks, for telling me how angry you are!" When others ask me to do something for them and I say, "No, I don't want to do that," they usually do not congratulate me for turning them down. Self-assertion is a lonely business. I have had no choice but to grow, however. Once I started to change, I knew that I did not want to go back to being depressed, hostile, and miserable.

I have become much more of a feeling person than I was before. And I am raising a feeling child. Sometimes I wish I were not. I can understand (although I do not agree with) parents who force their children to adapt to their wishes. It must be easier to have an adaptive child around than one who is continually expressing feelings. My little girl is exultant, silly, joyful, funny, loving, and tearing around when she is up. She is angry, yelling, tearful, hating, full of rage, and screaming when she is down. And she expresses her feelings vehemently. I am usually several jumps behind her, up when she is going down and by the time she is up I am still down.

But I would not want her to adapt and shut off her feelings. I know too well how long it takes to leave that adaptation behind and allow feelings to exist.

I do not want her to assume a mask and thereafter hide herself behind its rigid features. I want her to be able to respond as she feels. And I don't want her to feel that she has to rescue in order to survive. So far, at not quite six years of age, she expresses no need to rescue. The other day a friend of ours was teasing her; he accused her of causing his nightmare:

"If you hadn't wanted me to watch that scary T.V. program with you," he said, "I wouldn't have had that bad dream."

My daughter hesitated. "Tell him it's his problem," I prompted.

"That's your problem," she said, and went on, "You didn't have to come in to watch T.V. with me and if you had a bad dream, it's not my fault. It's yours!"

"You know, she's right!" our friend said, forgetting about teasing her.

I do not want her to be a hero-maker. I want her to be able to express her feelings straight out at the time she is feeling them. I want her to be able to do what feels right for her so she won't get sidetracked on all the dead-end roads and circuitous paths that I've taken. I want her to be able to feel her pain so that she doesn't carry it thereafter in her body. And I want her to be able to turn off any destructive messages in her head and substitute constructive permission messages that are appropriate for her. Above all, I want her to live a life in which her feelings count.

Our parents did not have such advantages. They were taught that feelings were not okay. They were forced to adapt by razor straps and switches; they were told that children had no rights. Our parents are not entirely at fault for teaching us only what they knew. They learned from their parents and their parents before them. They grew up in adult-centered families and they grew up fast. They learned to work to help the family survive. And sometimes they had to leave home while they were still young so that the rest could have enough food. They were not supposed to express feelings and opinions of their own; they were supposed to adapt for the good of the family.

Today we allow our children to be people. They may express

their thoughts and feelings. They may act their appropriate ages; they are no longer expected to be little grownups. They may engage in the serious business of play. They may grow at their own rates and in their own time. They may grow up to forgive their parents the many mistakes they have made, mistakes the parents made in ignorance of any other way to behave.

I am not suggesting that you discount your feelings by reminding you that our parents' society did not permit feelings. If you are angry at your parents, you have a right to your anger. You don't need to discount your anger by making excuses for your parents. You can be as angry at parents who died and left you as at those who were too poor to feed you properly. You can realize what their problems were on an intellectual level, while still allowing your feelings to exist.

If you have a great deal of anger stored up, you may accomplish nothing by merely telling your parents how you feel. Much of your anger is directed towards your parents of yesteryear whom you are still carrying around in your head. Your parents of today may not understand your anger; they may feel hurt. They will tell you they did the best they could, and they will be right; they probably did. You feel one way, they feel another, and you are both right. There is no right or wrong to feelings.

Rather than confront your parents with your old anger, you may (and you may not) want someone else, such as a therapist, to help you get rid of your archaic anger and hurt and appreciation—don't forget the appreciation. Often we have some appreciation for the same things in a parent that we resent. Then, after you express enough anger and cry out enough hurt and offer your belated appreciation you reach a level of forgiveness, or at least an acceptance of the past. You may begin to understand what they did and why they did it; your volcano of feelings erupts and releases you from pressure. And as this pressure lifts you reach not only a forgiveness of your parents, but also a forgiveness of yourself. You can forgive yourself for all the labels your parents accused you of being, for doing all the things they did not like, for all the mistakes they thought you made. You can forgive yourself for being You.

As I forgive my own parents, I hope that my daughter will forgive me. If I could I would take back the years and behave differently—spend more time with her, and be more relaxed and wiser about taking care of her. But I can't anymore than my parents could take back the years for me. The past is past, I can't change what happened then. All I can do now is to share my mistakes with my daughter, tell her about her painful experiences, and accept her anger. My sharing with her will be important. For, whatever she has felt is real within her. If I tried to whitewash my behavior or her experiences she would not understand the reasons for her feelings. She might even think that she has no right to her feelings or that she is crazy for feeling the way she does. So I need to share the truth with her, even if I hurt because of that sharing.

I remember a woman in a class of mine who told me how she was giving her baby the love and attention she never gave her ten- and twelve-year-old sons when they were infants.

"My older boys have asked me if I treated them like I do the baby," she said. "I know that I didn't. I was very harsh on them. But I don't want them to think that. So I've told them that I gave them every bit as much love. Am I doing the right thing?"

"No, you're not." I said. "You're doing exactly the wrong thing. You need to tell them about the rotten things you did. They already have their feelings. If you tell them the opposite to what they feel, they may think they're crazy. So, tell them the truth, even if it hurts. Corroborate their feelings. They may be angry at you today but they'll appreciate you for being straight in years to come."

The most loving, well-intentioned parent in the world still cannot satisfy all of an infant's needs. The child will still experience frustrations—wet diapers, tardy feedings, a parent who sleeps through his cries, dogs, bees, fevers, and colic. Even though the parents are straight about their feelings and about past events, that child may grow up with repressed, archaic pain. My consolation is that my daughter will have help in her quest for growth earlier than I did. When I was growing up there was little help around. Most of the tools for rapid change—Transactional Analysis, Gestalt, Behavior Modification, Psychodrama, Assertiveness Training, and the rest—have only been commonly available for the last fifteen or so years. If my daughter needs it, she will have help contacting her feelings and letting them go so that she will not waste years depressing herself or coping indirectly with her anger, as I did. Nor will she spend so much time defending against her feelings, or fighting the destructive forces built of those defenses.

Defenses are channels for release of pressure. When you tense yourself against pain, your tension causes pressure inside your body—sometimes enormous pressure. If that pressure is not released at the time by *ex*pression of feelings, *re*pression results. Then the pressure will have to be released later in the form of some defense. And what of your original tension? My daughter put it concisely to me when she was about five years old. One day I saw her biting her fingernails—her defense.

"How come you're biting your fingernails?" I asked her. "Are you tense?"

"What does tense mean?" she asked.

"What does tense mean?" I repeated. "I don't know, I've never thought about it. I guess it means uptight. What does tense mean to you?"

She thought about the question for a few moments. Then she said, "Tense means, 'I want my Mommy.' "

I gasped. She was right. That is the precise meaning for "tense" in my *now* understanding of the term. She was speaking not of the Mommy who was sitting right next to her, but of the Mommy of her infancy, the Mommy who failed to fulfill her basic needs. And because that Mommy did not satisfy her, she will feel her nebulous want inside of her, assigning it to this or to that, until she deals with the want itself in some way. She will not satisfy her want for long by biting her fingernails or by getting a new toy. She may relieve her tension for a little while, but the want will remain.

When we assign our wants to some defense we deal thereafter with the symptom, not the cause. We don't eliminate our basic wants when we take a cigarette or a drink, overeat or buy too many things. We release some of our tension so that we may cope with our lives, coping by destroying ourselves daily in small ways. But our basic want—our basic tension which creates our internal pressure—remains until we work on the want itself.

At times internal pressure may build so much that a person destroys himself or someone else, not over a lifetime but in a minute. Enough repressed tension can explode into suicide—or homicide—depending on how it is directed. If children direct their anger onto themselves because they have been taught to believe they are bad or stupid or good for nothing, or that they have no right to a place in this universe, they might try to erase their worthless selves out of existence. I am continually surprised at the numbers of people who have been taught that they are not okay and should not exist. Awhile ago at a workshop, I asked everyone who had *not* thought of committing suicide at one time or another to raise their hands. Out of twenty of us, two raised their hands.

Or, if children direct their anger at others, they might end up killing somebody. They might be models of behavior all their lives until one day the feelings explode. On that day they might act out their anger with a rifle or a knife, and some innocent person may die. Believing that others are to blame, their anger may erupt outwardly into homicide. Believing that others are out to get them and unaware of their projection, they may try to get others first.

We no longer need to repress our feelings and build elaborate defenses to hold them in. We are rapidly changing our old values and the old belief system which taught us to be tightly controlled. We are giving ourselves increasing permission to feel. Today men can cry without being "weak"; women can express their anger without being "unladylike." We can tell each other what we feel without being "bad." We no longer have to overeat, drink too much, fade out on drugs, work too hard, or kill ourselves in other ways, either slowly or in haste.

We no longer have to be right. It is unfortunate that we humans are rarely given the gift of foresight. Our powers of hindsight, however, are remarkable. We can easily discover the right decisions we should have made in retrospect, but when we make those decisions in the here and now it is not so easy. We need to allow ourselves to make mistakes. How else can we learn? Making mistakes is our human way of evaluating our performance. Mistakes are a vital part of the decision-making process. If we are so afraid of failure that we won't risk making a mistake, we will never accomplish anything. But if we can accept our own fallibility as an integral part of our learning mechanism, then we can use our failures as stepping stones to success.

Nor do we have to try to please everyone. Some people will dislike us, no matter how hard we try to please them. Whether or not we express our feelings straightforwardly or say what we think others want to hear, some will reject us. So why bother to manipulate? Why not come out straight with gut-level feelings? You and I both know that we hide our true feelings because of our old fear of being abandoned. Since we have survived childhood, we can now stop living our lives in fear of that abandonment. We who are alive today know we can survive. And because we know that we can survive we can stop repressing our feelings; we can stop limiting ourselves because of our fantasies of being rejected.

We can also stop trying hard at all. Our trying hard sets up such a strain within our bodies that we defeat ourselves from attaining our goals. How much more relaxing it is to simply do what we want to do without trying hard! How much easier it is to respond to others in the moment without trying so hard to control their responses! When we control others we are trying to get something from them—usually love and approval. We set up unattainable goals for ourselves. For we cannot force others to give us love any more than others can force us. No matter how hard others try, they cannot fill us with happiness or supply us with the love we never got from our parents. We can no longer get the love we did not receive then; we cannot go back to infancy. But we can accept what love others are able to give us in the here and now. We can give ourselves strokes in order to refuel our inner selves. And we can quit trying hard to manipulate others, to create defenses against our own pain, to hide our feelings.

Only through knowing what we feel can we know our real identities behind the roles we play. Only through our feelings can we know and appreciate being alive. Life is right here, right now. If we live in the future, filled with anxiety, or in the past, filled with depression, we are not deeply alive. Being in the moment, Now, is being alive. Feeling is being alive. We only have one life on this earth. Let's enjoy it, touch it through our five senses while we still can.

Let's get to know ourselves again, and through knowing our own feelings, to know others as well. Let's break down the barriers of isolation and alienation from one another. Let's break through to risk, to trust, to love. Join me. Drop the role that others have inflicted on you. Take off your mask. Open yourself to others with intimacy. Open yourself to your Self. Feel. Act Yourself.

Bibliography

BAKKER, CORNELIS B. and BAKKER-RABDAU, MARIANNE K. *No Trespassing, Explorations in Human Territoriality*, San Francisco, Chandler & Sharp Pub. Co., 1973.

BERNE, ERIC. *Transactional Analysis in Psychotherapy*, New York, Ballantine Books, Grove Press, 1961.

BLATNER, HOWARD. *Acting In: Practical Applications of Psychodramatic Methods*, New York, Springer Pub., 1973.

DEMAUSE, LLOYD. "Our Forebears Made Childhood a Nightmare," *Psychology Today*, April 1975, V. 8, No. 11.

DEMOS, JOHN. *A Little Commonwealth: Family Life in Plymouth Colony*, New York, Oxford University Press, 1970.

ELLIS, ALBERT and HARPER, ROBERT A. *A New Guide to Rational Living*, North Hollywood, California, 1975.

FLACH, FREDERIC. *The Secret Strength of Depression*, New York, Bantam Books, 1975.

FROST, ROBERT. *Complete Poems*, New York, Holt, Rinehart & Winston, 1964.

GREY, ZANE. *Riders of the Purple Sage*, Harper & Row, New York, 1912.

JANOV, ARTHUR. *The Primal Revolution*, New York, a Touchstone Book, Simon & Schuster, 1972.

KARPMAN, STEPHEN, "Fairy Tales and Script Drama Analysis," *Transactional Analysis Bulletin*, V. 7, San Francisco, California, 1968.

KELLY, GEORGE. *The Psychology of Personal Constructs*, New York, Norton Publishing Co., 1955.

LOWEN, ALEXANDER. *The Betrayal of the Body*, New York, Collier Books, Macmillan Pub. Co., Inc., 1967.

LYNES, RUSSEL. *The Domesticated Americans*, New York, Harper & Row, 1963.

OLSON, KEN. *The Art of Hanging Loose in an Uptight World*, Connecticut, Fawcett Books, 1974.

PERLS, FREDERICK S. *Gestalt Therapy Verbatim*, New York, Bantam Books, Real People Press, 1974.

SCHIFFMAN, MURIEL. *Gestalt Self Therapy and Further Techniques for Personal Growth*, Menlo Park, California, Bookpeople, Self Therapy Press, 1971.

STEINER, CLAUDE. *Scripts People Live: Transactional Analysis of Life Scripts*, New York, Grove Press, 1972.

VISCOTT, DAVID. *The Making of a Psychiatrist*, New York, Arbor House, 1972.

WATTS, ALAN. *The Wisdom of Insecurity*, New York, Vintage Books, Random House, Inc., 1951.

Webster's New World Dictionary of the American Language. David B. Guralink, Ed.-in-Chf. Second College Edition, Cleveland, Ohio, World Pub. Co., Inc., 1976.

Index